Scale 1: 500,000
or 8 miles to 1 inch
(5 km to 1 cm)

Reprinted with amendments January 2004
9th edition October 2003

© Automobile Association
Developments Limited 2004

 **Ordnance** This product includes mapping
Survey® data licensed from Ordnance
Survey® with the permission of the Controller of Her
Majesty's Stationery Office.

© Crown copyright 2004. All rights reserved.
Licence number 399221.

This product includes mapping
data licensed from Ordnance
Survey of Northern Ireland®
ORDNANCE SURVEY®
OF NORTHERN IRELAND reproduced by permission of the
Chief Executive, acting on behalf of the Controller of
Her Majesty's Stationery Office.

© Crown copyright 2004. Permit No.30204.

Republic of Ireland mapping based on Ordnance
Survey Ireland. Permit No. MP0003203.
© Ordnance Survey Ireland and
Government of Ireland.

All rights reserved. No part of this publication may
be reproduced, stored in a retrieval system, or
transmitted in any form or by any means –
electronic, mechanical, photocopying, recording or
otherwise – unless the permission of the publisher
has been given beforehand.

Published by AA Publishing (a trading name of
Automobile Association Developments Limited,
whose registered office is Millstream, Maidenhead
Road, Windsor, Berkshire SL4 5GD Registration
number 1878835).

Mapping produced by the Cartographic Department
of The Automobile Association.
This atlas has been compiled and produced from
the Automaps database utilising electronic and
computer technology (A02085).

ISBN 0 7495 3894 5 (standard bound)
ISBN 0 7495 3858 9 (wire bound)

A CIP Catalogue record for this book is available
from the British Library.

Printed in Britain by Scotprint, Haddington,
Scotland.

The contents of this atlas are believed to be correct
at the time of the latest revision. However, the
publishers cannot be held responsible for loss
occasioned to any person acting or refraining from
action as a result of any material in this atlas, nor for
any errors, omissions or changes in such material.
This does not affect your statutory rights. The
publishers would welcome information to correct
any errors or omissions and to keep this atlas up to
date. Please write to the Cartographic Editor,
Publishing Division, The Automobile Association,
Fanum House, Basing View, Basingstoke,
Hampshire RG21 4EA.

AA GLOVEBOX ATLAS

BRITAIN

Atlas contents

Map pages	II
Road map symbols	1
Road atlas Britain 1:500,000 scale	2–65
Mileage charts	68 & 92
Britain	68
Ireland	92
Index to places in Britain	66–84
County, administrative area map	66–67
Road atlas Ireland 1:1 million scale	85–91
In...	93–94

GW00417805

Map pages

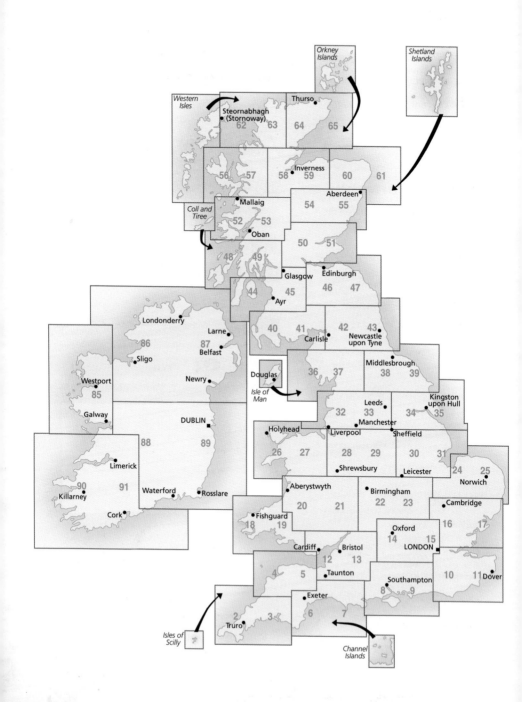

Orkney Islands

Shetland Islands

Western Isles

Thurso

Steornabhagh (Stornoway)
62 63 64 65

Inverness
56 57 58 59 60 61

Coll and Tiree

Mallaig Aberdeen
54 55

52 53
Oban

50 51

48 49

Glasgow Edinburgh
44 45 46 47
Ayr

Londonderry

Larne
86 87
Sligo Belfast

Carlisle Newcastle upon Tyne
40 41 42 43

Newry

Westport
85
Galway

Douglas
Isle of Man

Middlesbrough
36 37 38 39

88 89
DUBLIN

Leeds
Kingston upon Hull
32 33 34 35
Manchester
Holyhead Liverpool Sheffield

90 91
Limerick
Killarney Waterford Rosslare
Cork

26 27 28 29 30 31
Shrewsbury Leicester

24 25
Norwich

Aberystwyth Birmingham
20 21 22 23
Cambridge

18 19
Fishguard
16 17

Oxford
14 15
Cardiff Bristol LONDON
12 13

4 5 Taunton
10 11 Dover

Southampton
8 9

Exeter
2 3 6 7
Truro

Isles of Scilly

Channel Islands

Road map symbols

Britain

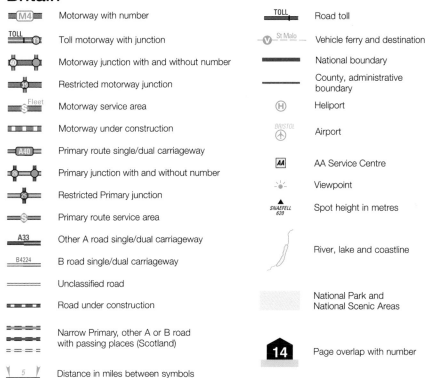

M4	Motorway with number
TOLL	Toll motorway with junction
	Motorway junction with and without number
39	Restricted motorway junction
Fleet	Motorway service area
	Motorway under construction
A40	Primary route single/dual carriageway
	Primary junction with and without number
25	Restricted Primary junction
S	Primary route service area
A33	Other A road single/dual carriageway
B4224	B road single/dual carriageway
	Unclassified road
	Road under construction
	Narrow Primary, other A or B road with passing places (Scotland)
5	Distance in miles between symbols

TOLL	Road toll
St Malo	Vehicle ferry and destination
	National boundary
	County, administrative boundary
H	Heliport
BRISTOL	Airport
AA	AA Service Centre
	Viewpoint
SNAEFELL 620	Spot height in metres
	River, lake and coastline
	National Park and National Scenic Areas
14	Page overlap with number

8 miles to 1 inch

1: 500 000

0   5   10 miles
0   5   10   15 kilometres

Ireland

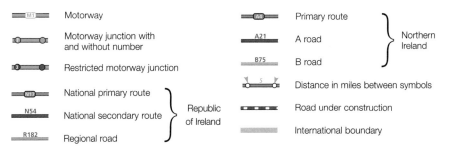

M1	Motorway
	Motorway junction with and without number
3	Restricted motorway junction
N17	National primary route
N54	National secondary route
R182	Regional road

Republic of Ireland

A4	Primary route
A21	A road
B75	B road

Northern Ireland

5	Distance in miles between symbols
	Road under construction
	International boundary

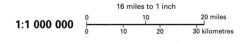

16 miles to 1 inch

1:1 000 000

0   10   20 miles
0   10   20   30 kilometres

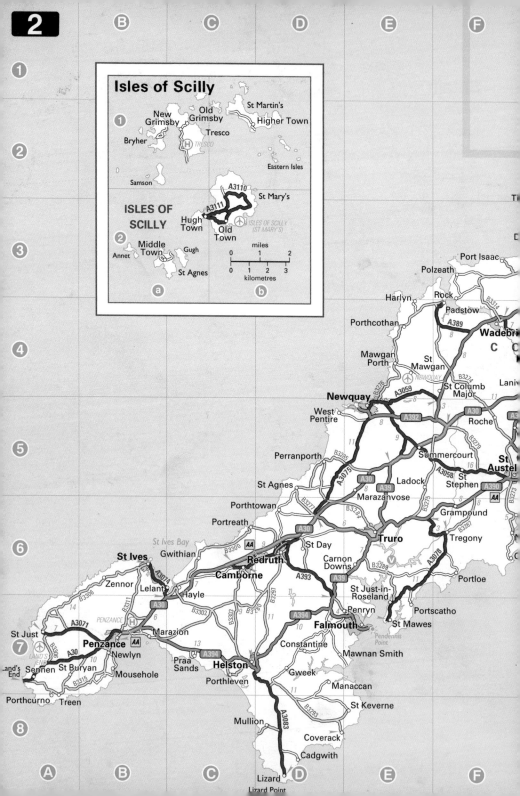

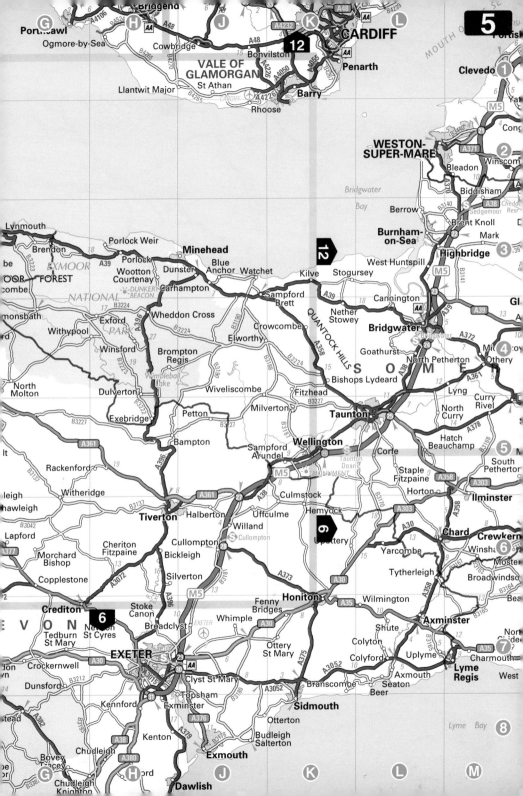

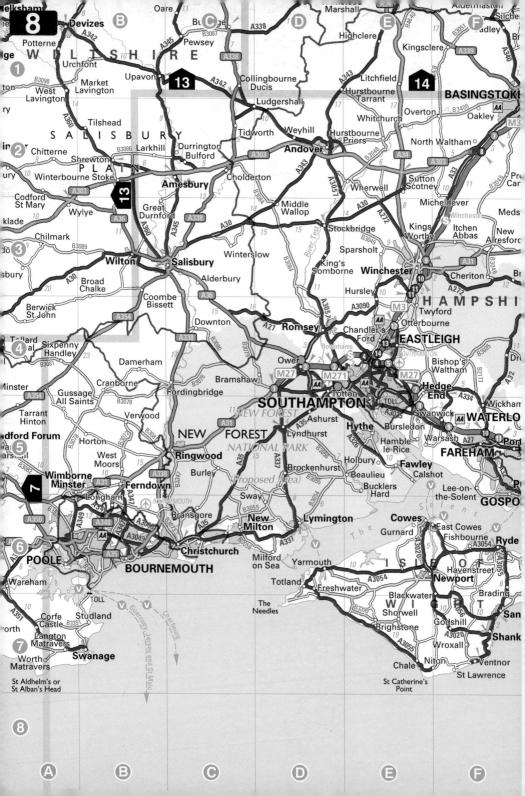

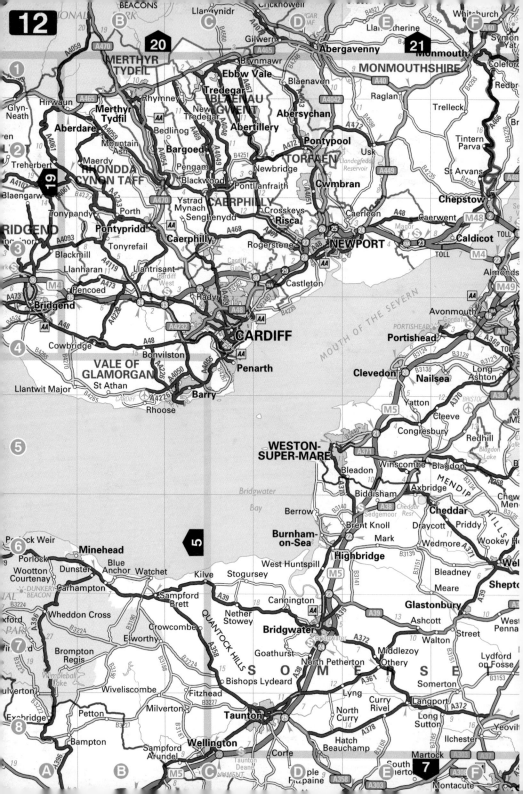

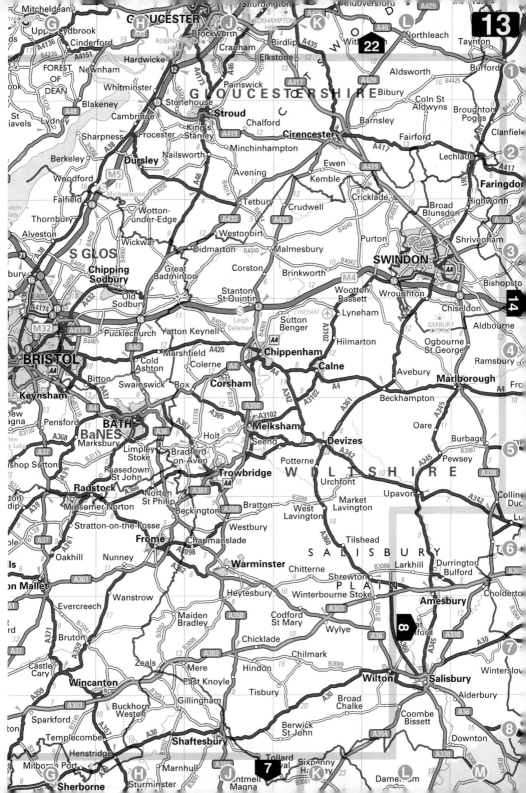

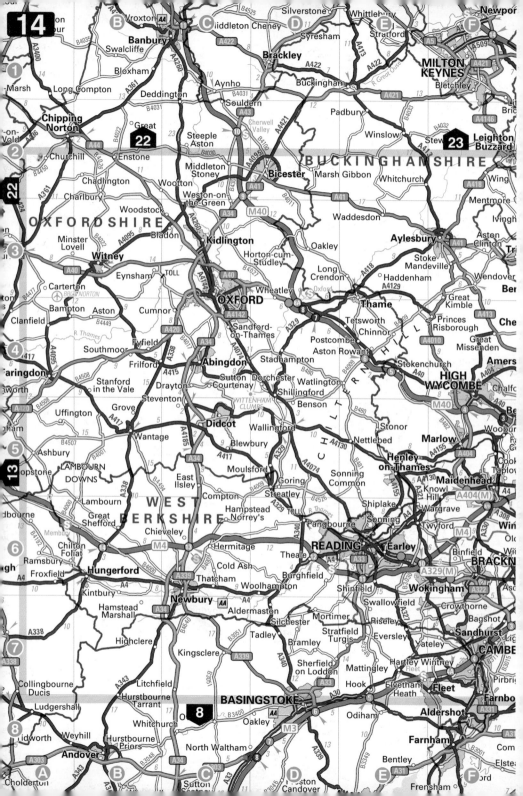

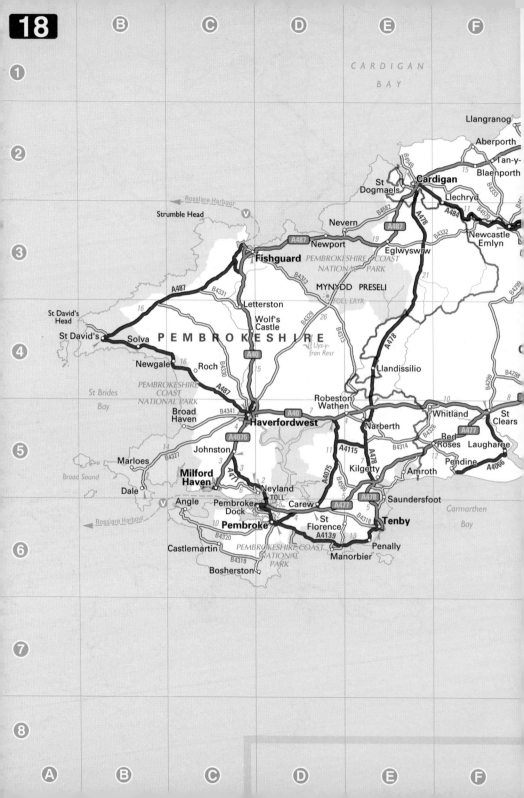

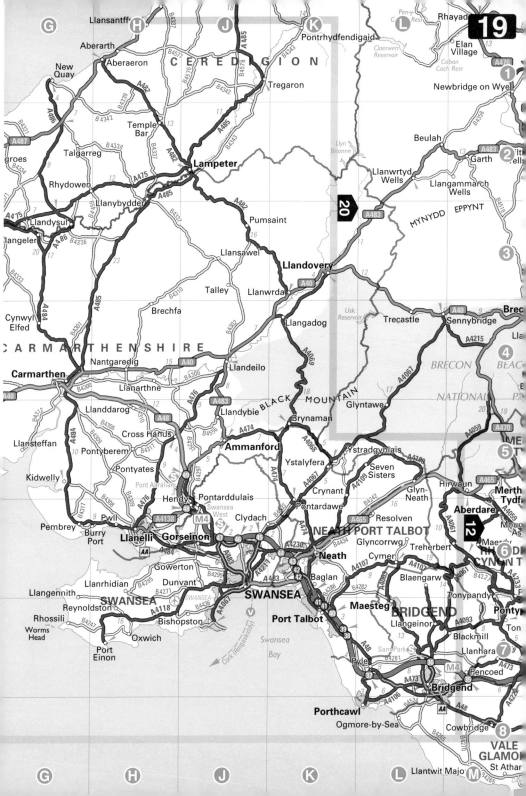

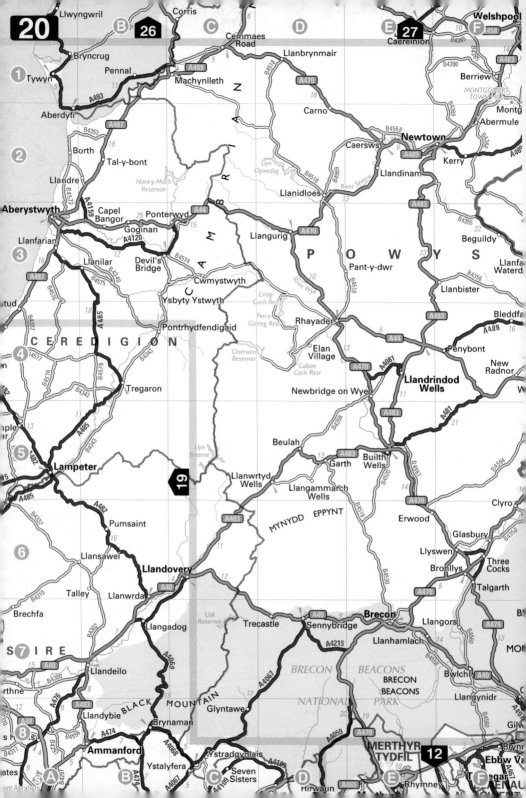

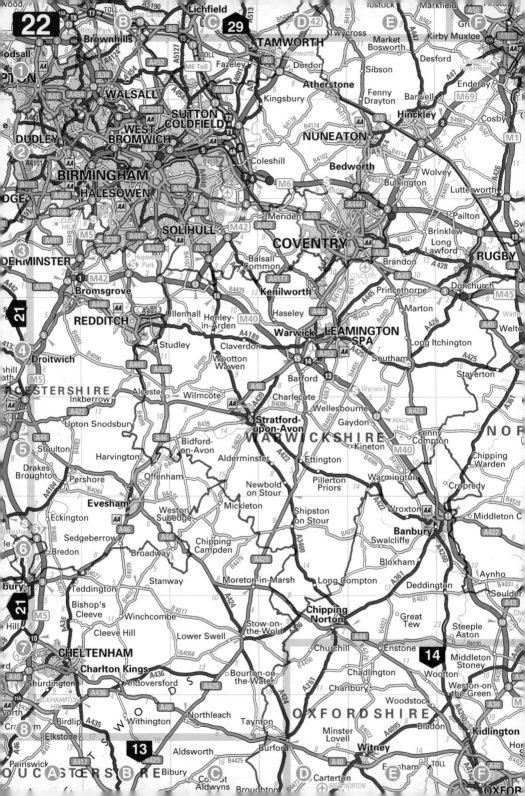

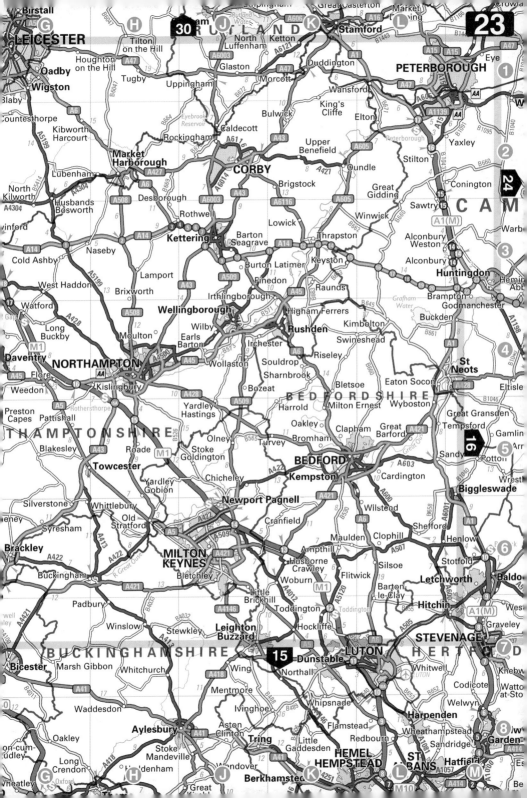

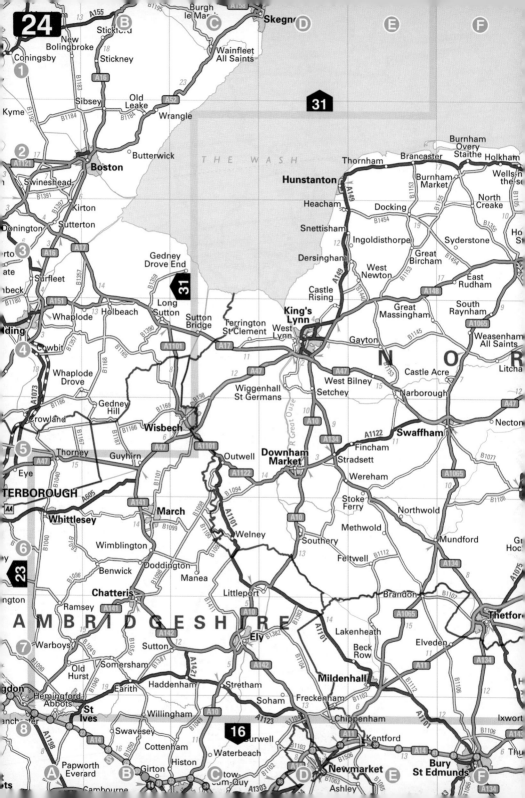

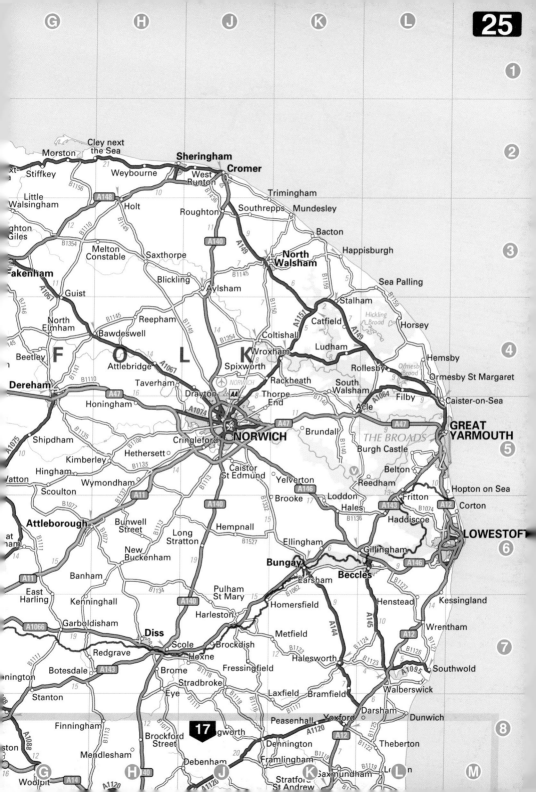

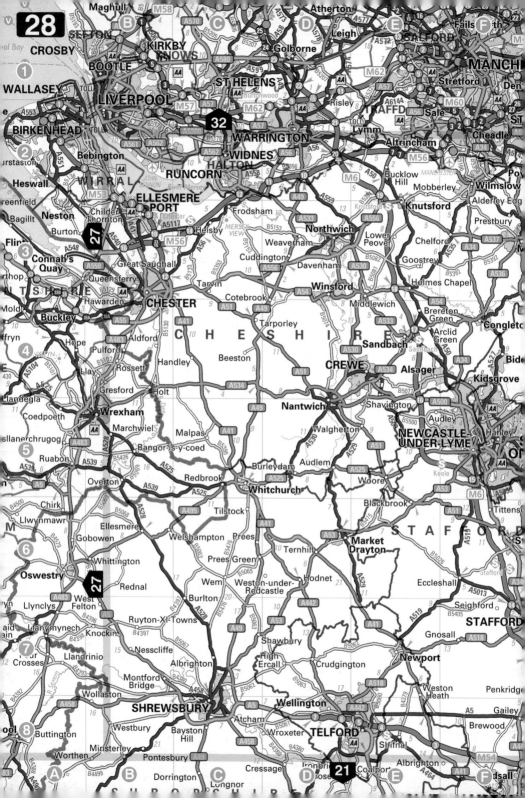

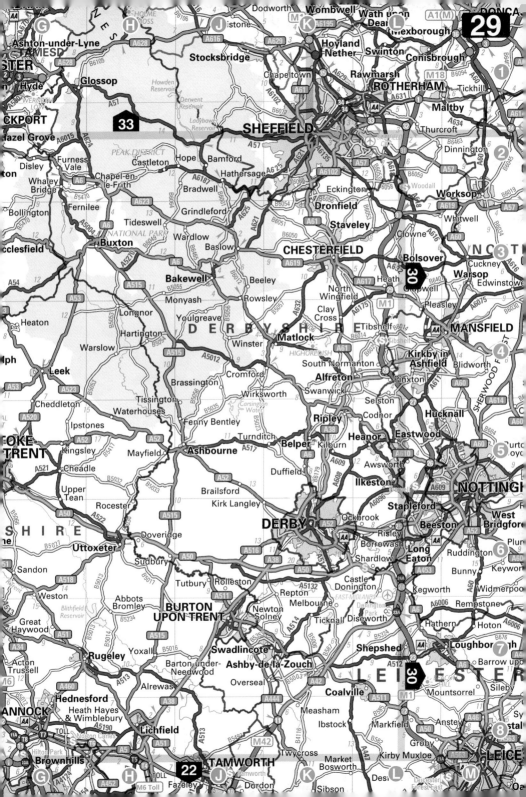

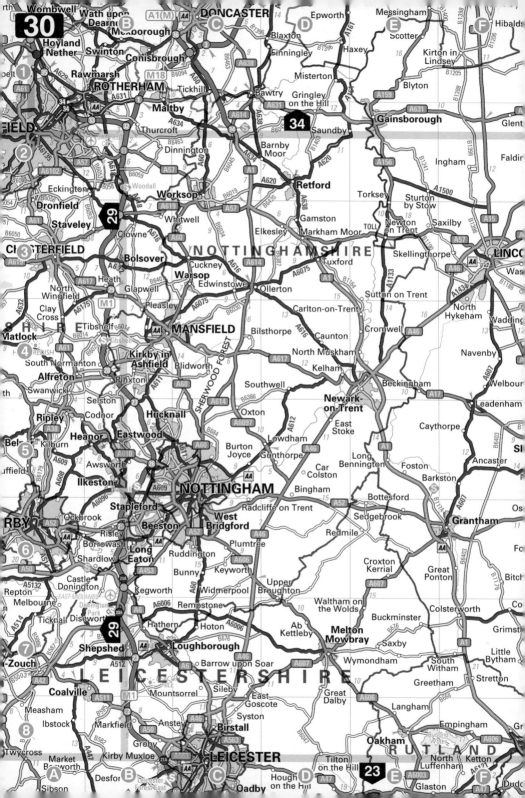

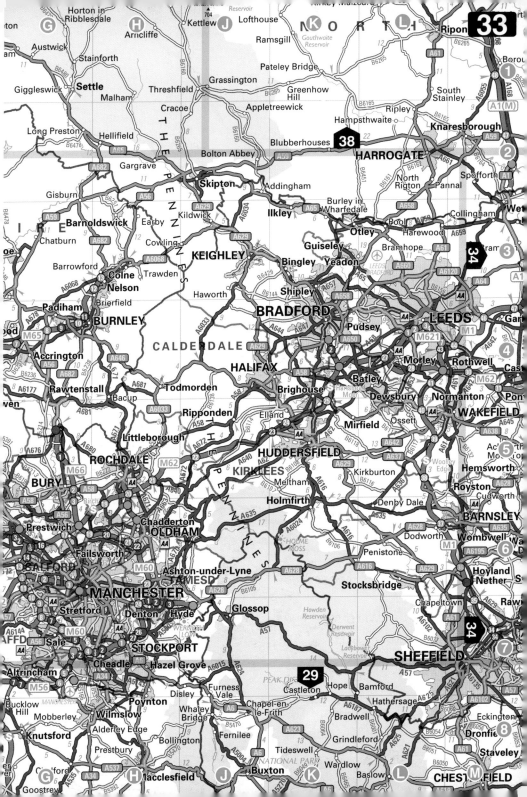

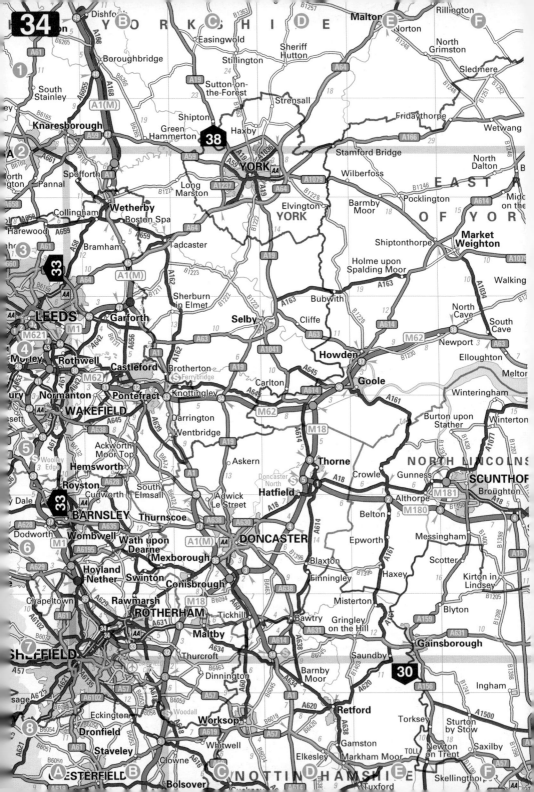

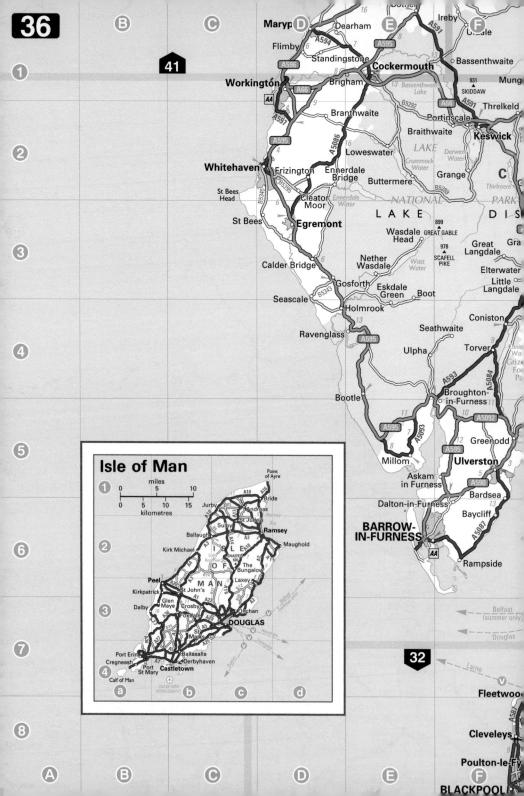

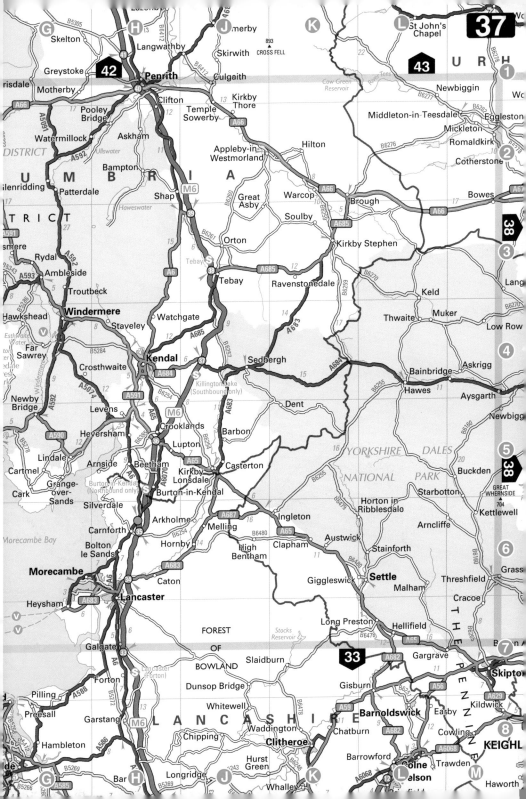

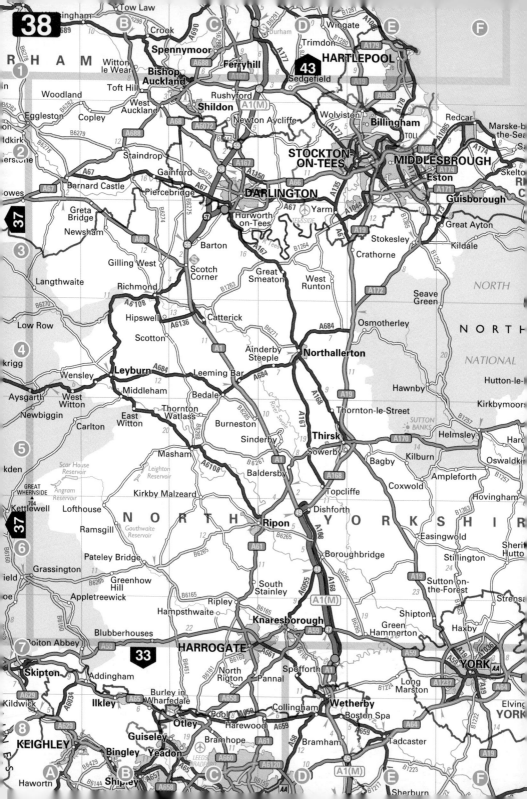

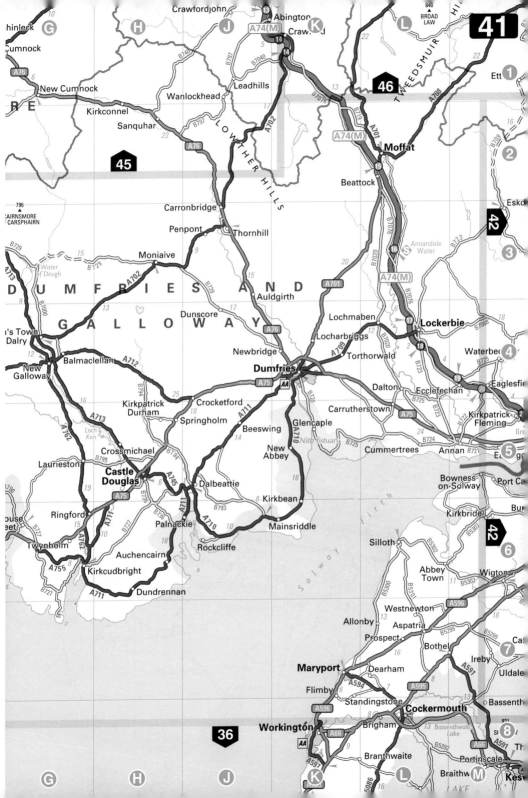

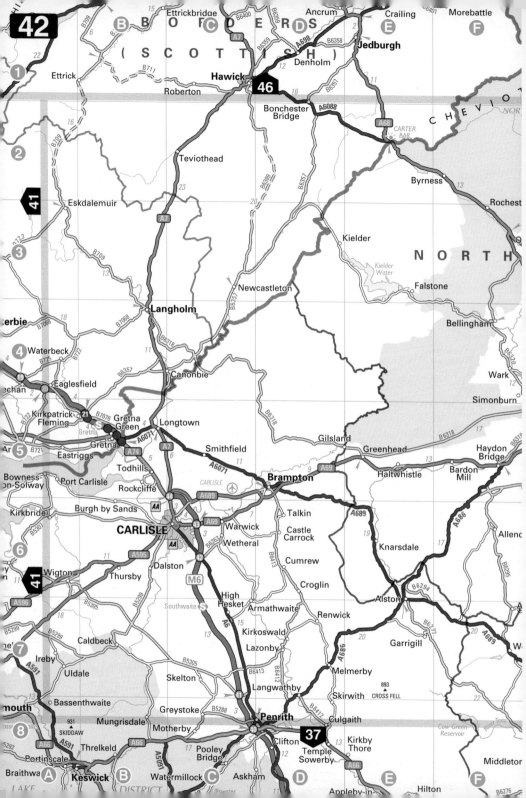

B · C · D · E · F

1

Otter Ferry · Glendaruel · Blairmore · Kilcreggan
B836 · A880
Kilfinan · Sandbank · Strone
A8003 · Dunoon · Gourd
7 Kyles · A815
of · Inverkip
Bute · A70 · A7
Colintraive · INVER
Kames
Portavadie · Port · Skelmorlie
Bannatyne · A886
Bute · Rothesay · A844
A64 · Ascog · A841
Great · Millport · Largs
Cumbrae · Kilchattan · A78 · NO
Island

2

Kilberry
B8024 · A83
Kennacraig
Whitehouse

Tarbert
Skipness
Claonaig · B001
Clachan · B842
Loch · Garasdale · B8001

Fairlie
A78

3

Gigha
Ardminish
A83

West
Kilbride · B781 · B780
AYRS

Tayinloan

Lochranza · North Arran · 8
Corrie · 874 · GOATFELL
ARRAN · A841
B880 · 11 · Brodick
Dippen · Carradale · 17 · A841
Glenbarr · Saddell
Bellochantuy · Torbeg · Lamlash
K I N T Y R E · Blackwaterfoot · Whiting Bay
16 · A841

Ardrossan
Saltcoats
A738
Kilwi

4

5

A83 · Kilkenzie
CAMPBELTOWN · Campbeltown
achrihanish · B843 · 6
B842 · 10

Belfast

6

Dunure
A719
Maybe
Turnberry · Kirkos
12

ull of · Southend
tyre
Sanda
Island

7

Ailsa Craig

· A77
Girvan · A

8

Lendalfoot · 13
A77 · B734
Colmonell · 9
Ballantrae · Pinwherry
B704 · Barrhi

A · B · C · D · E · F

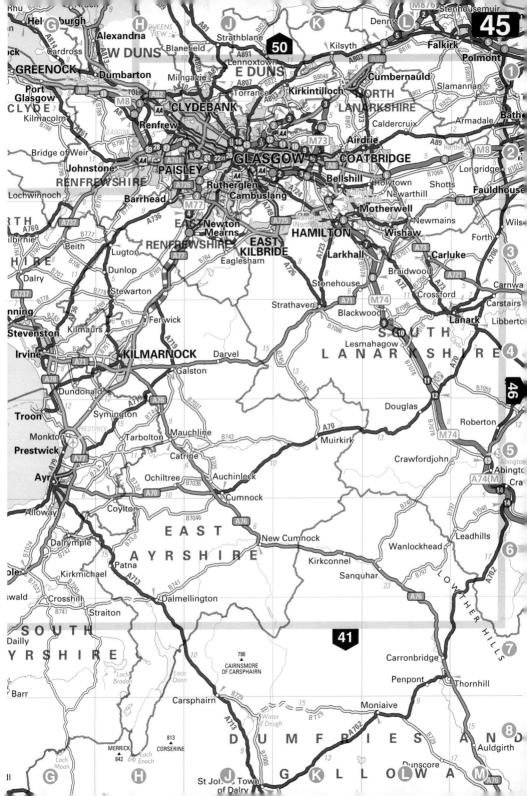

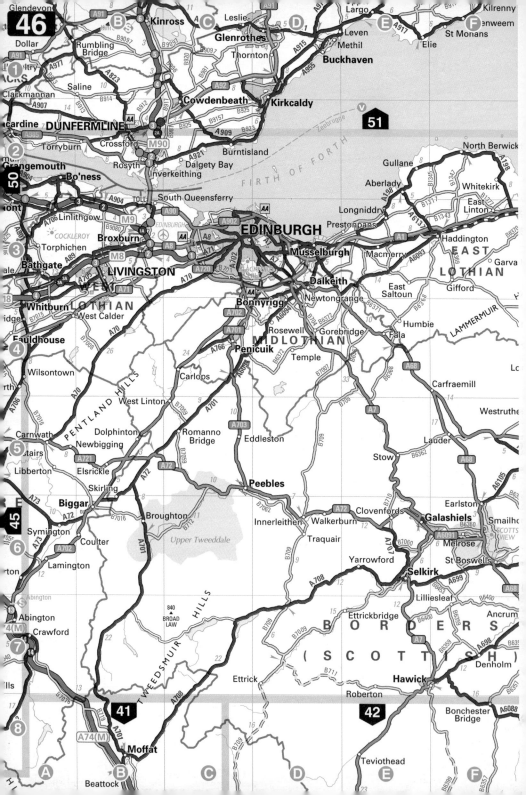

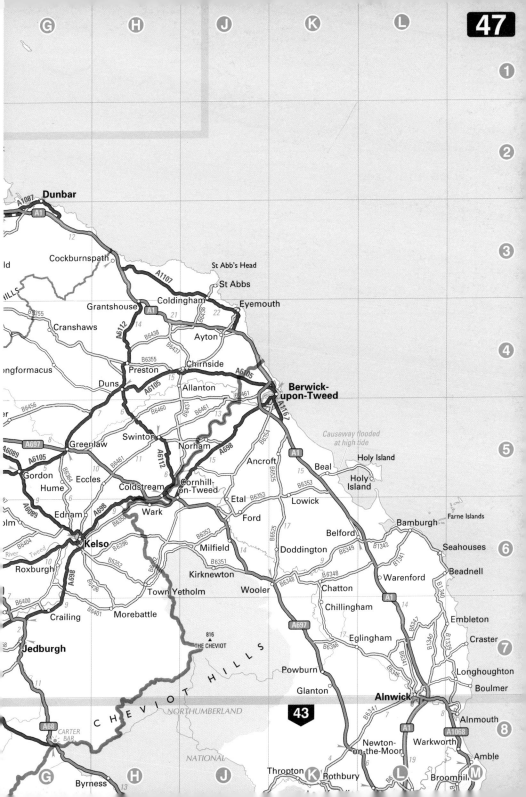

G   H   J   K   L

1
2
3
4
5
6
7
8

Dunbar
A1087
A1
12
Cockburnspath
A1107
St Abb's Head
St Abbs
Grantshouse
Coldingham
Eyemouth
A1
HILLS
B6355
21
22
B6438
Cranshaws
A6112
14
B6438
Ayton
B6437
B6355
Chirnside
ngformacus
Preston
Duns
A6105
15
A6605
Allanton
B6461
Berwick-
upon-Tweed
A1167
B6456
A6105
7
6
B6460
B6437
B6461
13
B6354
Causeway flooded
at high tide
A697
Greenlaw
Swinton
Norham
A698
Ancroft
Beal
A1
Holy Island
A6089
A6105
5
B6461
11
A6112
15
B6525
Holy
Island
Gordon
B6364
10
6
612
Cornhill-
on-Tweed
Lowick
B6353
Farne Islands
Eccles
Hume
Coldstream
Etal
B6353
Bamburgh
A6089
6
Ednam
A698
9
Wark
Ford
B6525
17
Belford
Seahouses
Kelso
B6396
B6352
Milfield
Doddington
9
B6349
B7342
B1341
Beadnell
Roxburgh
River Tweed
10
B6352
Kirknewton
14
B6351
Warenford
B1340
Embleton
B6400
B6404
2
B6436
Town Yetholm
B6348
Wooler
B6348
Chatton
A1
14
B6347
Craster
Crailing
B6401
Morebattle
Chillingham
B1339
Longhoughton
Jedburgh
816
THE CHEVIOT
Eglingham
B1340
B6341
Boulmer
11
Powburn
B6346
Alnwick
7
CHEVIOT HILLS
NORTHUMBERLAND
43
Glanton
B6341
A1
8
A68
CARTER
BAR
NATIONAL
Newton-
on-the-Moor
A1068
Warkworth
A1
19
8
G   H   J   K   L   M
Byrness
Thropton
Rothbury
B6
Broomhill
Amble

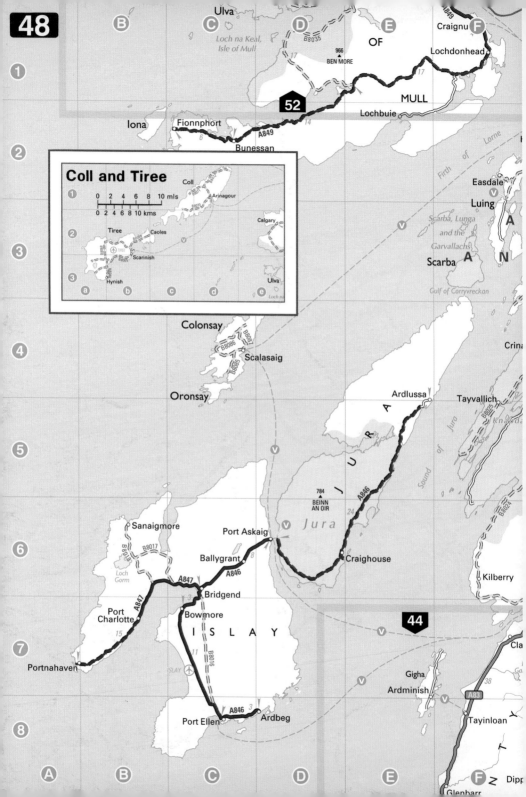

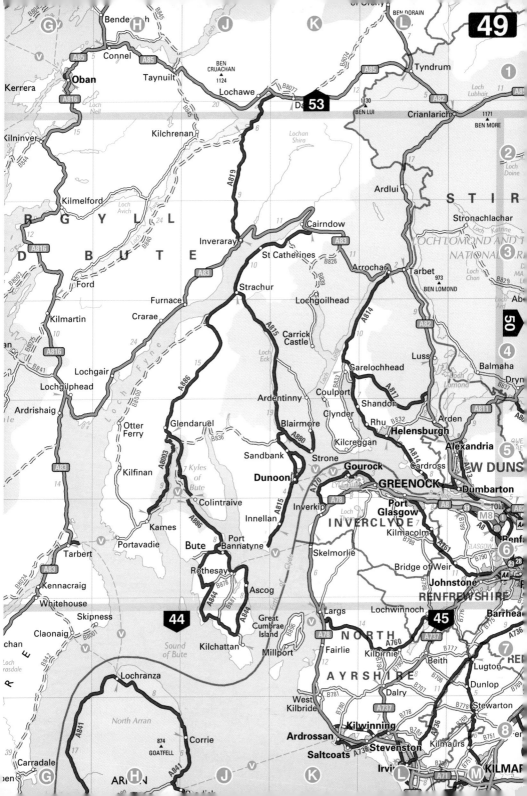

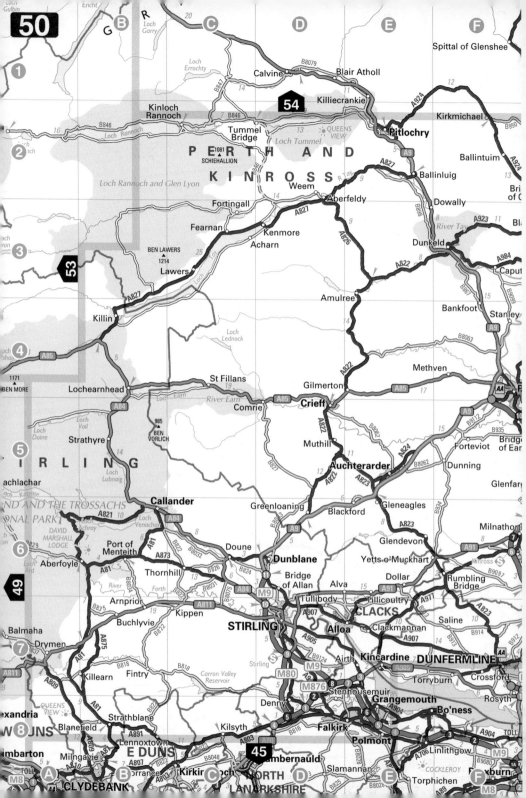

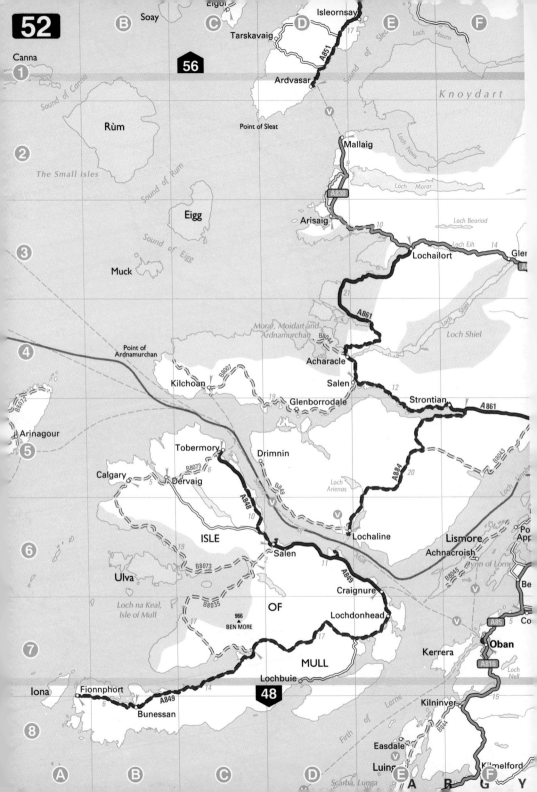

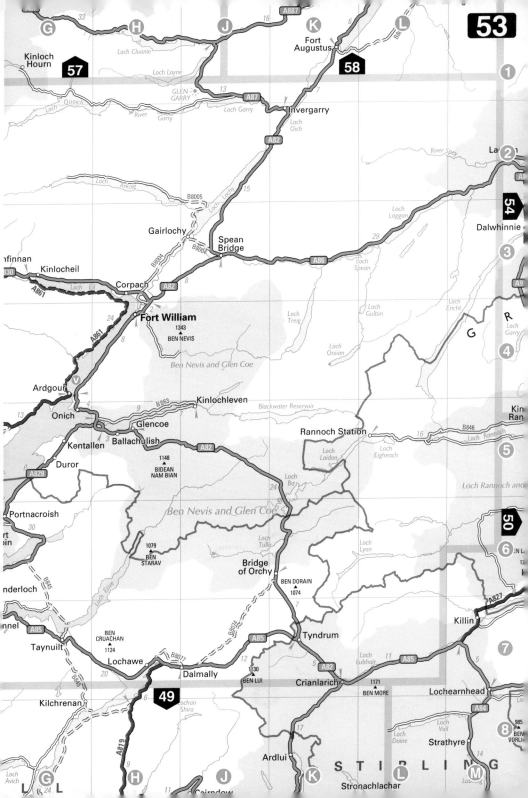

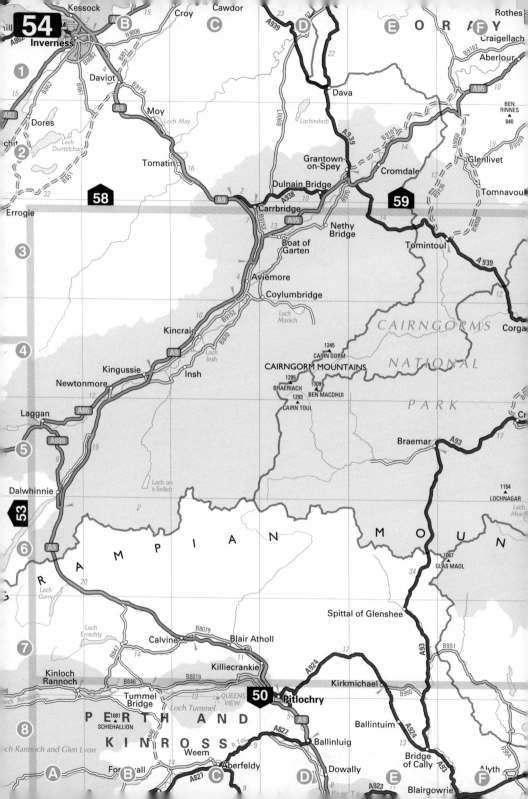

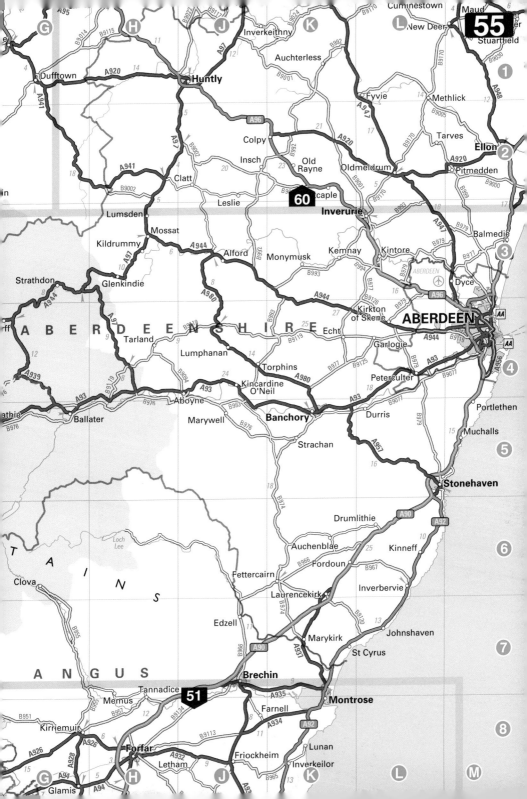

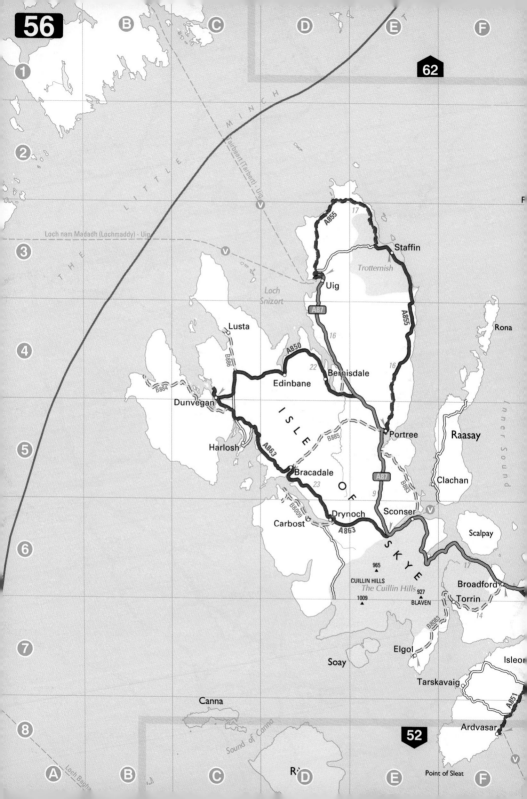

A · B · C · D · E · F

1

62

2

LITTLE · MINCH

Tairbeart (Tarbert) - Uig

Loch nam Madadh (Lochmaddy) - Uig

3

THE

V

V

Staffin

Trotternish

Uig

A855

17

Loch Snizort

A87

16

Rona

A855

Lusta

B886

4

A850

22

Bernisdale

16

Edinbane

B884

Dunvegan

ISLE

Portree

Raasay

Harlosh

A863

B885

5

Inner Sound

Bracadale

23

Clachan

OF

A87

9

B883

Sconser

V

Carbost

B8009

Drynoch

Scalpay

6

A863

SKYE

17

965

CUILLIN HILLS

The Cuillin Hills

927

Broadford

1009

BLAVEN

Torrin

7

B8083

14

Elgol

Isleor

Soay

Tarskavaig

Canna

A851

8

52

Ardvasar

V

A · B · C · D · E · F

Loch Baghar

Sound of Canna

Ri

Point of Sleat

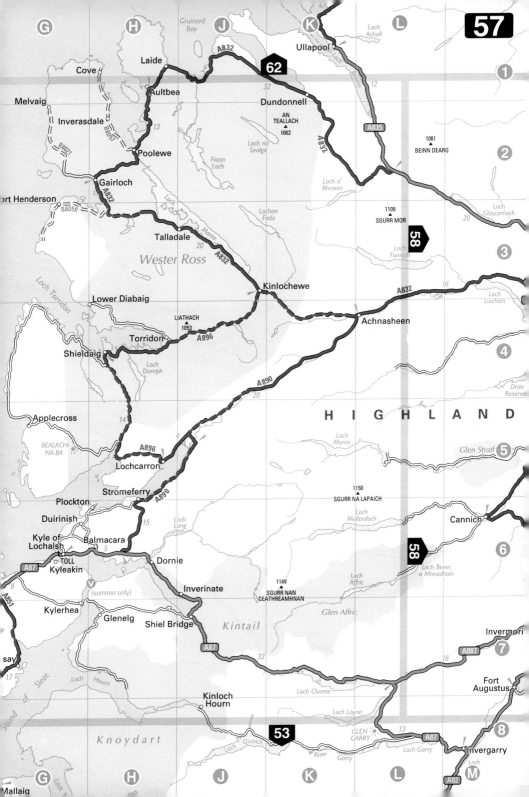

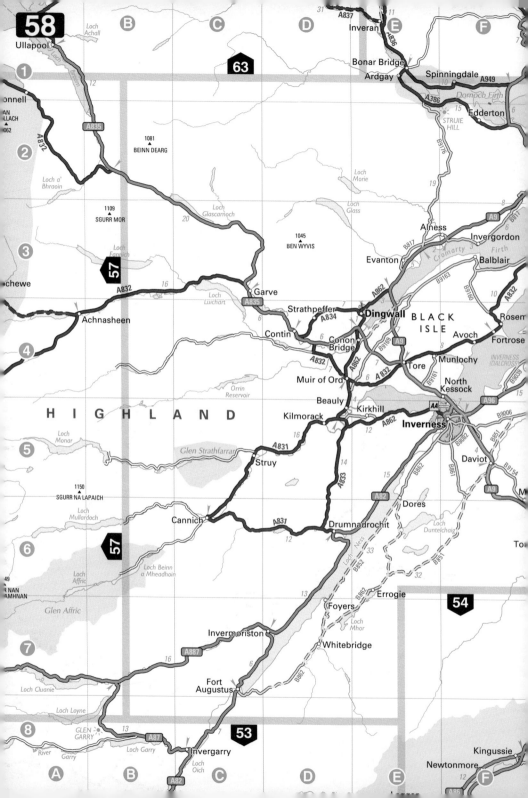

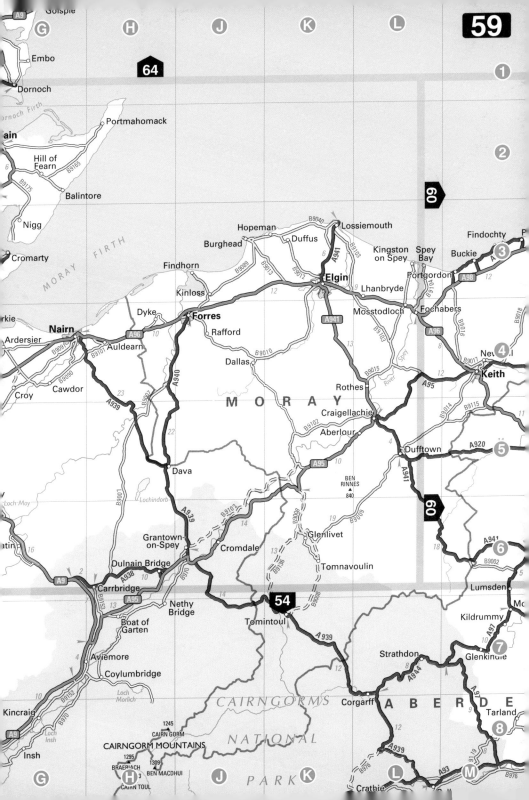

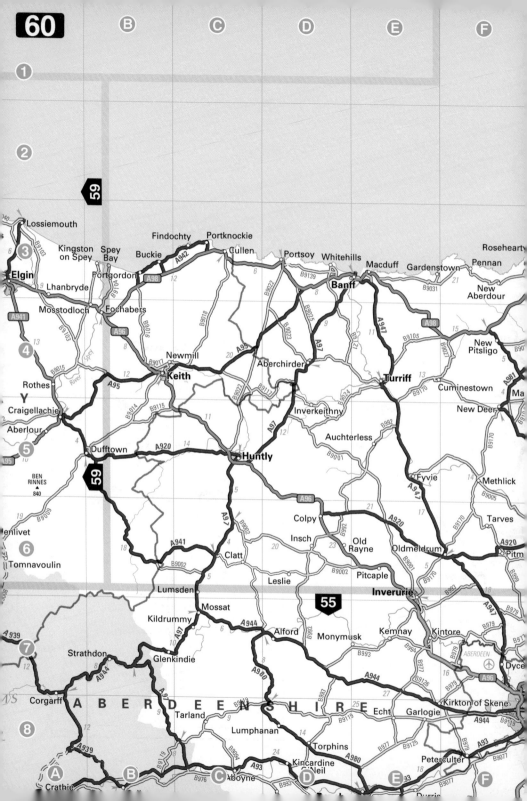

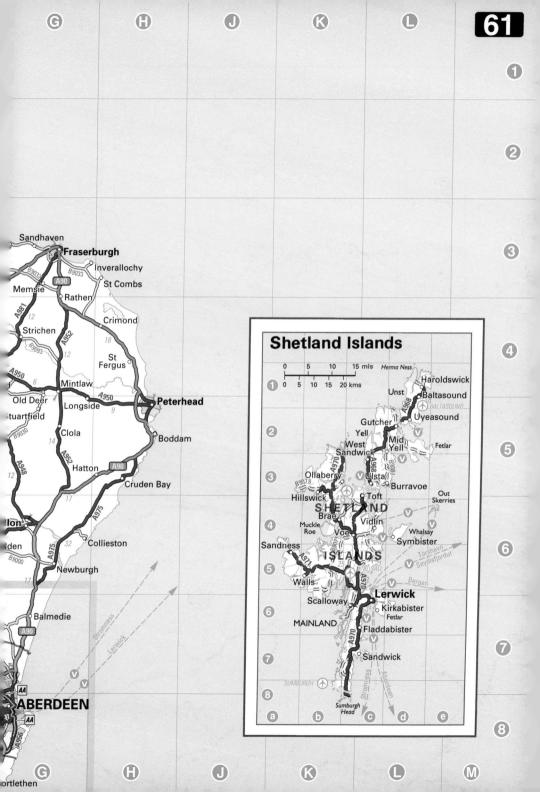

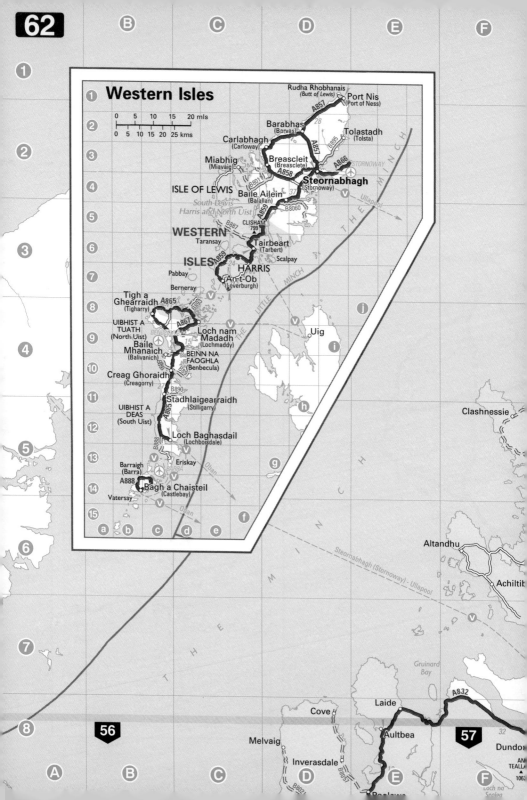

Western Isles

Rudha Rhobhanais
(Butt of Lewis)
Port Nis
(Port of Ness)
A857

Barabhas
(Barvas)
Tolastadh
(Tolsta)
Carlabhagh
(Carloway)
A857
A859
Breascleit
(Breasclete)
A858
Miabhig
(Miavaig)
Steornabhagh
(Stornaway)
A866
STORNOWAY

ISLE OF LEWIS
Baile Ailein
(Balallan)
A859
V
Ullapool
South Lewis
Harris and North Uist
B8060

WESTERN
CLISHAM
799
B887
Taransay
Tairbeart
(Tarbert)
A859
Scalpay

ISLES
HARRIS
An t-Ob
(Leverburgh)
Pabbay
Berneray
V

Tigh a
Ghearraidh
(Tigharry)
A865
A867
V
UIBHIST A
TUATH
(North Uist)
BENBECULA
Loch nam
Madadh
(Lochmaddy)
V
Uig
i
j
Baile
Mhanaich
(Balivanich)
BEINN NA
FAOGHLA
(Benbecula)
Creag Ghoraidh
(Creagorry)
A865
B890
Stadhlaigearraidh
(Stilligarry)
h
UIBHIST A
DEAS
(South Uist)
A865
g
Loch Baghasdail
(Lochboisdale)
B888
Barraigh
(Barra)
Eriskay
Oban
A888
Bagh a Chaisteil
(Castlebay)
Vatersay
V
Oban
f

a   b   c   d   e

Clashnessie

Altandhu
Achiltib
V

Steornabhagh (Stornoway) - Ullapool

Gruinard
Bay
Laide
A832
Cove
Aultbea
Dundo
Melvaig
Inverasdale
AN
TEALLA
1062
Loch na
Sgalea

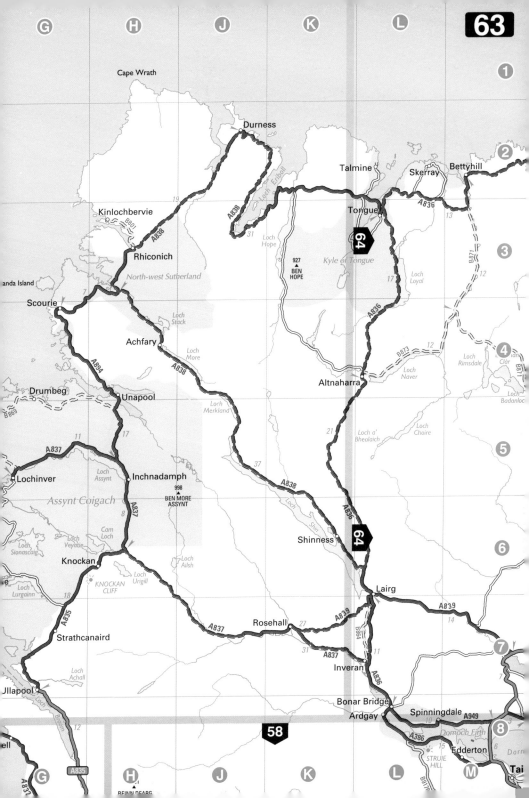

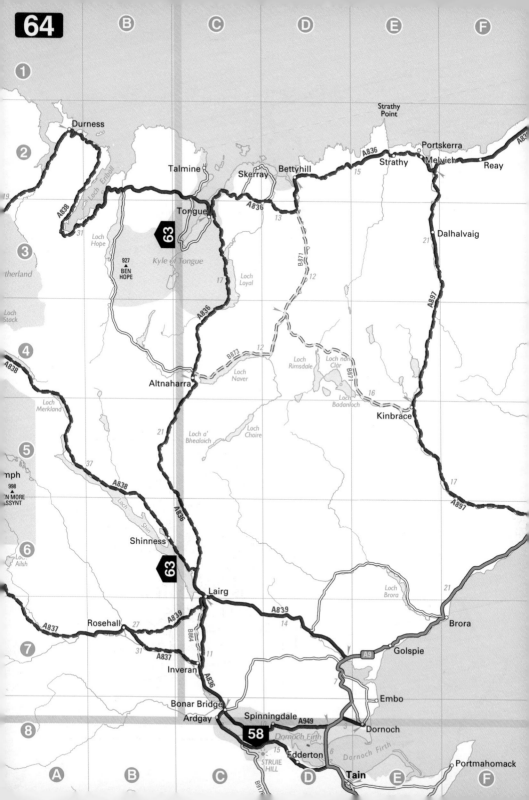

G H J K L

1
2
3
4
5
6
7
8

Scrabster
Thurso
16
5
Dunnet Head
Dunnet
Gills 15 A836 John O'Groats
Duncansby Head
Freswick
Castletown
B876 16 A99
Keiss
Loch Calder
B874
Halkirk
A9
B874
B874
17
Loch Shurrery
B870
Spittal
Watten B874
A882
21
WICK
Wick
Loch More
Thrumster
A99
A9
17
Latheron
Lybster
Dunbeath
20
Berriedale
A9
Helmsdale

Orkney Islands

Mull Head
North Ronaldsay
Pierowall
Papa Westray
Westray B9064
Midbea Rapness
Sanday B9064
Calfsound
Braeswick
Wasbister
Rousay Eday
Brough Head
A966 Brinyan Backaland
ORKNEY Stronsay
Dounby Hackland Shapinsay
MAINLAND Finstown Balfour
A967 ISLANDS **Kirkwall**
Stromness A964 KIRKWALL
Rora Head A960
Houton St Mary's
HOY Scapa Burray
Lyness Flotta Flow St Margaret's Hope
South Ronaldsay
A961 Burwick
PENTLAND FIRTH

0 5 10 mls
0 5 10 15 kms

a b c d

G H J K L M

Index to places in Britain

This index lists places appearing in the main-map section of the atlas in alphabetical order. The reference before each name gives the atlas page number and grid reference of the square in which the place appears. The map shows counties, unitary authorities and administrative areas, together with a list of the abbreviated name forms used in the index.

England

BaNES	**Bath & N E Somerset (18)**
Barns	**Barnsley (19)**
Beds	**Bedfordshire**
Birm	**Birmingham**
Bl w D	**Blackburn with Darwen (20)**
Bmouth	**Bournemouth**
Bolton	**Bolton (21)**
Bpool	**Blackpool**
Brad	**Bradford (22)**
Br & H	**Brighton and Hove (23)**
Br For	**Bracknell Forest (24)**
Bristl	**City of Bristol**
Bucks	**Buckinghamshire**
Bury	**Bury (25)**
C Derb	**City of Derby**
C KuH	**City of Kingston upon Hull**
C Leic	**City of Leicester**
C Nott	**City of Nottingham**
C Pete	**City of Peterborough**
C Plym	**City of Plymouth**
C Port	**City of Portsmouth**
C Sotn	**City of Southampton**
C Stke	**City of Stoke**
Calder	**Calderdale (26)**
Cambs	**Cambridgeshire**
Ches	**Cheshire**
Cnwll	**Cornwall**
Covtry	**Coventry**
Cumb	**Cumbria**
Darltn	**Darlington (27)**
Derbys	**Derbyshire**
Devon	**Devon**
Donc	**Doncaster (28)**
Dorset	**Dorset**
Dudley	**Dudley (29)**
Dur	**Durham**
E R Yk	**East Riding of Yorkshire**
E Susx	**East Sussex**
Essex	**Essex**
Gatesd	**Gateshead (30)**
Gloucs	**Gloucestershire**
Gt Lon	**Greater London**
Halton	**Halton (31)**
Hants	**Hampshire**
Hartpl	**Hartlepool (32)**
Herefs	**Herefordshire**
Herts	**Hertfordshire**
IoS	**Isles of Scilly**
IoW	**Isle of Wight**
Kent	**Kent**
Kirk	**Kirklees (33)**
Knows	**Knowsley (34)**
Lancs	**Lancashire**
Leeds	**Leeds**
Leics	**Leicestershire**
Lincs	**Lincolnshire**
Lpool	**Liverpool**
Luton	**Luton**
M Keyn	**Milton Keynes**
Manch	**Manchester**
Medway	**Medway**

Middsb	**Middlesbrough**
NE Lin	**North East Lincolnshire**
N Linc	**North Lincolnshire**
N Som	**North Somerset (35)**
N Tyne	**North Tyneside (36)**
N u Ty	**Newcastle upon Tyne**
N York	**North Yorkshire**
Nhants	**Northamptonshire**
Norfk	**Norfolk**
Notts	**Nottinghamshire**
Nthumb	**Northumberland**
Oldham	**Oldham (37)**
Oxon	**Oxfordshire**
Poole	**Poole**
R & Cl	**Redcar and Cleveland**
Readg	**Reading**
Rochdl	**Rochdale (38)**
Rothm	**Rotherham (39)**
Rutlnd	**Rutland**
S Glos	**South Gloucestershire (40)**
S on T	**Stockton-on-Tees (41)**
S Tyne	**South Tyneside (42)**
Salfd	**Salford (43)**
Sandw	**Sandwell (44)**
Sefton	**Sefton (45)**
Sheff	**Sheffield**
Shrops	**Shropshire**
Slough	**Slough (46)**
Solhll	**Solihull (47)**
Somset	**Somerset**
St Hel	**St Helens (48)**
Staffs	**Staffordshire**
Sthend	**Southend-on-Sea**
Stockp	**Stockport (49)**
Suffk	**Suffolk**
Sundld	**Sunderland**
Surrey	**Surrey**
Swindn	**Swindon**
Tamesd	**Tameside (50)**
Thurr	**Thurrock (51)**
Torbay	**Torbay**
Traffd	**Trafford (52)**
W & M	**Windsor & Maidenhead (53)**
W Berk	**West Berkshire**
W Susx	**West Sussex**
Wakefd	**Wakefield (54)**
Warrtn	**Warrington (55)**
Warwks	**Warwickshire**
Wigan	**Wigan (56)**
Wilts	**Wiltshire**
Wirral	**Wirral (57)**
Wokham	**Wokingham (58)**
Wolves	**Wolverhampton (59)**
Worcs	**Worcestershire**
Wrekin	**Telford and Wrekin (60)**
Wsall	**Walsall (61)**
York	**York**

Channel Islands & Isle of Man

Guern	**Guernsey**
Jersey	**Jersey**
IoM	**Isle of Man**

Scotland

Abers	**Aberdeenshire**
Ag & B	**Argyll & Bute**
Angus	**Angus**
Border	**Borders**
C Aber	**City of Aberdeen**
C Dund	**City of Dundee**
C Edin	**City of Edinburgh**
C Glas	**City of Glasgow**
Clacks	**Clackmannanshire (1)**
D & G	**Dumfries & Galloway**
E Ayrs	**East Ayrshire**
E Duns	**East Dunbartonshire (2)**
E Loth	**East Lothian**
E Rens	**East Renfrewshire (3)**
Falk	**Falkirk**
Fife	**Fife**
Highld	**Highland**
Inver	**Inverclyde (4)**
Mdloth	**Midlothian (5)**
Moray	**Moray**
N Ayrs	**North Ayrshire**
N Lans	**North Lanarkshire (6)**
Ork	**Orkney Islands**
P & K	**Perth & Kinross**
Rens	**Renfrewshire (7)**
S Ayrs	**South Ayrshire**
Shet	**Shetland Islands**
S Lans	**South Lanarkshire**
Stirlg	**Stirling**
W Duns	**West Dunbartonshire (8)**
W Isls	**Western Isles**
W Loth	**West Lothian**

Wales

Blae G	**Blaenau Gwent (9)**
Brdgnd	**Bridgend (10)**
Caerph	**Caerphilly (11)**
Cardif	**Cardiff**
Carmth	**Carmarthenshire**
Cerdgn	**Ceredigion**
Conwy	**Conwy**
Denbgs	**Denbighshire**
Flints	**Flintshire**
Gwynd	**Gwynedd**
IoA	**Isle of Anglesey**
Mons	**Monmouthshire**
Myr Td	**Merthyr Tydfil (12)**
Neath	**Neath Port Talbot (13)**
Newpt	**Newport (14)**
Pembks	**Pembrokeshire**
Powys	**Powys**
Rhondd	**Rhondda Cynon Taff (15)**
Swans	**Swansea**
Torfn	**Torfaen (16)**
V Glam	**Vale of Glamorgan (17)**
Wrexhm	**Wrexham**

Mileage chart - Britain

The mileage chart shows distances in miles between two towns along AA-recommended routes. Using motorways and other main roads this is normally the fastest route, though not necessarily the shortest.

Lincoln - Sheffield = 47 miles

1 mile = 1.6 kilometres

Aberdeen
Aberystwyth
Barnstaple
Birmingham
Brighton
Bristol
Cambridge
Cardiff
Carmarthen
Dorchester
Dover
Edinburgh
Exeter
Fort William
Glasgow
Gloucester
Guildford
Holyhead
Hull
Inverness
Kendal
Leeds
Lincoln
Liverpool
Maidstone
Manchester
Middlesbrough
Newcastle
Norwich
Nottingham
Oxford
Penzance
Perth
Plymouth
Sheffield
Southampton
Stranraer
Taunton
Wick
York
LONDON

```
472
608 214
436 124 180
613 288 210 171
518 130 100 90 169
463 215 267 97 120 170
537 111 128 109 202 44 203
236 236 371 199 376 281 256 300
520 48 190 172 264 107 266 68 284
600 206 94 172 119 62 184 120 364 182
587 326 272 208 82 205 124 239 381 301 200
126 336 471 299 476 381 333 400 100 386 463 458
593 198 44 165 178 84 259 113 356 175 57 248 455
156 435 570 398 576 480 456 499 199 485 562 580 137 554
150 332 467 295 472 377 353 396 96 382 459 477 47 451 102
484 113 126 56 155 36 150 63 248 125 118 192 346 110 445 343
571 224 175 128 44 106 96 139 335 201 97 97 433 150 532 430 99
464 102 339 167 345 249 259 202 228 150 331 369 326 323 425 323 215 302
376 227 320 139 258 230 138 250 170 311 312 262 247 304 367 266 196 239 218
106 496 631 459 637 541 517 561 260 546 623 641 157 616 66 176 507 595 488 430
283 189 324 153 330 234 251 254 47 240 316 354 145 309 245 143 200 288 181 164 307
329 173 301 120 262 211 146 230 123 224 293 271 200 285 321 179 177 220 165 59 383 110
388 199 275 98 216 185 95 205 182 267 246 220 258 260 379 277 151 173 204 44 441 176 74
362 110 272 101 278 182 193 202 126 158 264 302 224 257 324 222 148 236 102 128 386 79 74 139
545 284 234 166 50 167 82 200 339 262 161 41 416 209 537 435 153 58 327 220 599 313 231 178 261
357 134 261 89 266 171 160 190 120 184 253 290 219 245 318 216 136 224 125 97 380 74 44 85 34 248
276 244 357 176 318 267 197 286 95 294 349 322 146 341 283 190 232 276 235 89 308 84 64 122 145 280 114
235 275 388 207 349 298 229 317 60 325 380 353 106 372 242 153 264 307 266 142 267 102 95 154 176 311 145 39
488 278 329 160 168 233 63 266 282 328 241 172 359 313 480 378 212 160 321 147 542 276 174 103 240 130 185 223 254
395 162 232 51 193 142 86 161 189 223 224 210 266 216 387 285 107 151 178 93 449 164 77 39 112 168 71 130 161 119
510 160 170 68 109 73 82 107 274 169 115 146 373 154 472 370 48 67 242 190 534 228 174 132 176 107 164 227 258 146 102
702 308 108 274 287 193 368 222 466 284 167 357 564 109 663 562 220 259 434 415 726 419 403 370 367 318 356 451 482 433 326 265
86 388 523 351 529 433 378 453 152 438 515 503 42 507 102 64 399 486 379 291 114 199 245 303 278 461 275 192 150 404 310 426 617
633 239 62 205 218 124 299 153 397 215 98 288 495 44 594 493 151 190 365 346 657 350 334 301 298 249 287 382 413 364 257 196 78 544
397 166 272 91 233 182 122 201 261 263 264 247 236 256 359 257 149 191 157 66 421 115 38 47 79 205 39 100 131 148 45 142 366 309 297
578 225 142 135 66 106 136 140 342 201 53 152 440 111 539 437 100 49 309 258 601 295 241 199 243 113 232 294 325 204 169 67 221 489 152 209
235 342 477 305 482 387 363 406 106 392 469 487 132 461 181 86 352 440 333 276 261 153 229 288 232 445 229 201 163 388 295 380 571 149 502 267 447
560 165 50 132 160 51 226 80 323 142 45 224 422 34 521 419 77 126 291 272 583 277 261 228 225 185 213 309 340 291 184 123 144 471 75 224 94 429
207 597 732 560 738 642 618 662 361 647 724 742 258 716 166 277 608 695 588 531 104 408 484 543 487 700 484 409 367 644 550 635 826 215 757 523 702 362 684
323 201 314 133 275 224 154 243 116 251 306 279 193 298 314 212 189 233 192 38 376 91 24 79 102 237 71 51 89 180 87 184 408 239 357 57 251 223 265 477
550 239 216 121 54 120 59 153 314 215 125 78 413 200 512 410 102 31 282 186 574 268 201 143 216 39 204 254 285 118 129 56 310 462 241 169 77 420 167 675 211
```

A

30	D7	**Ab Kettleby** Leics
21	L4	**Abberley** Worcs
41	L6	**Abbey Town** Cumb
29	H7	**Abbots Bromley** Staffs
19	H1	**Aberaeron** Cerdgn
19	H1	**Aberarth** Cerdgn
60	D4	**Aberchirder** Abers
12	B2	**Aberdare** Rhondd
26	B6	**Aberdaron** Gwynd
55	M4	**Aberdeen** C Aber
20	A2	**Aberdyfi** Gwynd
50	D2	**Aberfeldy** P & K
26	C3	**Aberffraw** IOA
50	B6	**Aberfoyle** Stirlg
21	G8	**Abergavenny** Mons
27	H3	**Abergele** Conwy
46	E2	**Aberlady** E Loth
59	L5	**Aberlour** Moray
20	F2	**Abermule** Powys
51	G5	**Abernethy** P & K
18	F2	**Aberporth** Cerdgn
26	C6	**Abersoch** Gwynd
12	D2	**Abersychan** Torfn
12	D2	**Abertillery** Blae G
20	A3	**Aberystwyth** Cerdgn
14	C4	**Abingdon** Oxon
45	M5	**Abington** S Lans
55	J4	**Aboyne** Abers
16	D7	**Abridge** Essex
33	G4	**Accrington** Lancs
52	D4	**Acharacle** Highld
50	C3	**Acharn** P & K
63	H4	**Achfary** Highld
62	F6	**Achiltibuie** Highld
52	F6	**Achnacroish** Ag & B
57	L4	**Achnasheen** Highld
34	B5	**Ackworth Moor Top** Wakefd
25	K5	**Acle** Norfk
29	G7	**Acton Trussell** Staffs
33	J2	**Addingham** Brad
34	C6	**Adwick Le Street** Donc
38	D4	**Ainderby Steeple** N York
45	L2	**Airdrie** N Lans
50	E7	**Airth** Falk
28	C7	**Albrighton** Shrops
21	L1	**Albrighton** Shrops
9	K2	**Albury** Surrey
22	B4	**Alcester** Warwks
23	M3	**Alconbury** Cambs
23	L3	**Alconbury Weston** Cambs
14	A6	**Aldbourne** Wilts
35	J3	**Aldbrough** E R Yk
17	M2	**Aldeburgh** Suffk
8	C3	**Alderbury** Wilts
28	F3	**Alderley Edge** Ches
14	D7	**Aldermaston** W Berk
22	D5	**Alderminster** Warwks
9	H2	**Aldershot** Hants
28	B4	**Aldford** Ches
17	G5	**Aldham** Essex
13	L1	**Aldsworth** Gloucs
49	M5	**Alexandria** W Duns
9	K3	**Alfold** Surrey
55	J3	**Alford** Abers
31	K3	**Alford** Lincs
29	L4	**Alfreton** Derbys
10	D7	**Alfriston** E Susx
11	K4	**Alkham** Kent
47	H4	**Allanton** Border
42	F6	**Allendale** Nthumb
42	F7	**Allenheads** Nthumb
21	J6	**Allensmore** Herefs
50	E7	**Alloa** Clacks
41	L7	**Allonby** Cumb

45	G6	**Alloway** S Ayrs
13	G3	**Almondsbury** S Glos
58	F3	**Alness** Highld
43	K2	**Alnmouth** Nthumb
47	L7	**Alnwick** Nthumb
29	J7	**Alrewas** Staffs
28	E4	**Alsager** Ches
42	E6	**Alston** Cumb
62	F6	**Altandhu** Highld
34	E5	**Althorpe** N Linc
64	C4	**Altnaharra** Highld
9	G2	**Alton** Hants
7	K2	**Alton Pancras** Dorset
28	E2	**Altrincham** Traffd
50	E6	**Alva** Clacks
13	G3	**Alveston** Gloucs
51	G3	**Alyth** P & K
9	K4	**Amberley** W Susx
43	K2	**Amble** Nthumb
37	G3	**Ambleside** Cumb
15	G4	**Amersham** Bucks
8	C2	**Amesbury** Wilts
26	D1	**Amlwch** IOA
19	J5	**Ammanford** Carmth
38	F5	**Ampleforth** N York
23	K6	**Ampthill** Beds
18	E5	**Amroth** Pembks
50	E3	**Amulree** P & K
67	a2	**An t-Ob** W Isls
30	F5	**Ancaster** Lincs
47	K5	**Ancroft** Nthumb
47	G7	**Ancrum** Border
8	D2	**Andover** Hants
22	B7	**Andoversford** Gloucs
36	c1	**Andreas** IOM
18	C6	**Angle** Pembks
9	K5	**Angmering** W Susx
41	M5	**Annan** D & G
43	J6	**Annfield Plain** Dur
30	C8	**Anstey** Leics
31	G5	**Anwick** Lincs
37	J2	**Appleby-in-Westmorland** Cumb
57	G5	**Applecross** Highld
4	D4	**Appledore** Devon
11	H5	**Appledore** Kent
38	A7	**Appletreewick** N York
51	L3	**Arbroath** Angus
28	E4	**Arclid Green** Ches
49	L5	**Arden** Ag & B
49	K4	**Ardentinny** Ag & B
59	G4	**Ardersier** Highld
64	C8	**Ardgay** Highld
53	C4	**Ardgour** Highld
10	C5	**Ardingly** W Susx
17	H4	**Ardleigh** Essex
49	L2	**Ardlui** Ag & B
48	E4	**Ardlussa** Ag & B
44	A3	**Ardminish** Ag & B
49	G5	**Ardrishaig** Ag & B
44	F4	**Ardrossan** N Ayrs
52	D1	**Ardvasar** Highld
40	C7	**Ardwell** D & G
48	d1	**Arinagour** Ag & B
52	D3	**Arisaig** Highld
37	J6	**Arkholme** Lancs
45	M2	**Armadale** W Loth
42	C7	**Armathwaite** Cumb
37	M6	**Arncliffe** N York
50	B7	**Arnprior** Stirlg
37	H5	**Arnside** Cumb
16	B3	**Arrington** Cambs
49	L3	**Arrochar** Ag & B
9	K5	**Arundel** W Susx
49	J6	**Ascog** Ag & B
15	G6	**Ascot** W & M
11	K3	**Ash** Kent
29	J5	**Ashbourne** Derbys
6	B5	**Ashburton** Devon
14	A5	**Ashbury** Oxon
29	K7	**Ashby-de-la-Zouch** Leics

12	E7	**Ashcott** Somset
11	H4	**Ashford** Kent
43	K3	**Ashington** Nthumb
9	L4	**Ashington** W Susx
16	E2	**Ashley** Cambs
33	H6	**Ashton-under-Lyne** Tamesd
8	D5	**Ashurst** Hants
4	D7	**Ashwater** Devon
36	F5	**Askam in Furness** Cumb
34	C5	**Askern** Donc
37	H2	**Askham** Cumb
37	M4	**Askrigg** N York
41	L7	**Aspatria** Cumb
14	B4	**Aston** Oxon
14	F3	**Aston Clinton** Bucks
21	H3	**Aston on Clun** Shrops
14	E4	**Aston Rowant** Oxon
28	C8	**Atcham** Shrops
22	D1	**Atherstone** Warwks
32	F6	**Atherton** Wigan
25	G6	**Attleborough** Norfk
25	H4	**Attlebridge** Norfk
35	H2	**Atwick** E R Yk
55	K6	**Auchenblae** Abers
41	H6	**Auchencairn** D & G
45	J5	**Auchinleck** E Ayrs
50	E5	**Auchterarder** P & K
60	E5	**Auchterless** Abers
51	G5	**Auchtermuchty** Fife
28	D5	**Audlem** Ches
28	E5	**Audley** Staffs
59	H4	**Auldearn** Highld
41	J3	**Auldgirth** D & G
57	H1	**Aultbea** Highld
37	K6	**Austwick** N York
13	L4	**Avebury** Wilts
13	J2	**Avening** Gloucs
6	A6	**Aveton Gifford** Devon
54	C3	**Aviemore** Highld
58	F4	**Avoch** Highld
12	F4	**Avonmouth** Bristl
30	B5	**Awsworth** Notts
12	E5	**Axbridge** Somset
6	F3	**Axminster** Devon
6	F3	**Axmouth** Devon
14	F3	**Aylesbury** Bucks
11	K3	**Aylesham** Kent
25	J3	**Aylsham** Norfk
22	F6	**Aynho** Nhants
45	G5	**Ayr** S Ayrs
38	A4	**Aysgarth** N York
47	J4	**Ayton** Border

B

65	d2	**Backaland** Ork
25	K3	**Bacton** Norfk
33	H4	**Bacup** Lancs
38	E5	**Bagby** N York
62	b14	**Bagh a Chaisteil** W Isls
27	K3	**Bagillt** Flints
19	K6	**Baglan** Neath
14	F7	**Bagshot** Surrey
62	c10	**Baile a Mhanaich** W Isls
62	g4	**Baile Ailein** W Isls
37	M4	**Bainbridge** N York
34	F2	**Bainton** E R Yk
29	J3	**Bakewell** Derbys
27	H6	**Bala** Gwynd
62	g4	**Balallan** W Isls
51	G4	**Balbeggie** P & K
58	F3	**Balblair** Highld
10	B5	**Balcombe** W Susx
38	D5	**Baldersby** N York
16	B4	**Baldock** Herts
65	c3	**Balfour** Ork

59	G2	**Balintore** Highld
62	c10	**Balivanich** W Isls
53	H5	**Ballachulish** Highld
40	B4	**Ballantrae** S Ayrs
36	b4	**Ballasalla** IOM
55	G5	**Ballater** Abers
36	c2	**Ballaugh** IOM
50	E2	**Ballinluig** P & K
50	F2	**Ballintuim** P & K
48	C6	**Ballygrant** Ag & B
57	H6	**Balmacara** Highld
41	G4	**Balmaclellan** D & G
49	M4	**Balmaha** Stirlg
55	M3	**Balmedie** Abers
22	D3	**Balsall Common** Solhll
16	E3	**Balsham** Cambs
61	d1	**Baltasound** Shet
32	E4	**Bamber Bridge** Lancs
47	L6	**Bamburgh** Nthumb
29	J2	**Bamford** Derbys
37	H2	**Bampton** Cumb
5	H5	**Bampton** Devon
14	A4	**Bampton** Oxon
22	E6	**Banbury** Oxon
55	K5	**Banchory** Abers
60	E3	**Banff** Abers
26	E3	**Bangor** Gwynd
28	B5	**Bangor-is-y-coed** Wrexhm
25	H6	**Banham** Norfk
50	F4	**Bankfoot** P & K
10	B3	**Banstead** Surrey
62	h2	**Barabhas** W Isls
37	J5	**Barbon** Cumb
31	G3	**Bardney** Lincs
42	F5	**Bardon Mill** Nthumb
36	F5	**Bardsea** Cumb
22	D4	**Barford** Warwks
12	C2	**Bargoed** Caerph
16	C8	**Barking** Gt Lon
30	F5	**Barkston** Lincs
16	C4	**Barkway** Herts
16	C4	**Barley** Herts
34	E2	**Barmby Moor** E R Yk
26	E7	**Barmouth** Gwynd
39	L7	**Barmston** E R Yk
38	A2	**Barnard Castle** Dur
30	D2	**Barnby Moor** Notts
15	J4	**Barnet** Gt Lon
35	G6	**Barnetby le Wold** N Linc
33	H3	**Barnoldswick** Lancs
33	M6	**Barnsley** Barns
13	L2	**Barnsley** Gloucs
4	E4	**Barnstaple** Devon
40	D3	**Barr** S Ayrs
43	G4	**Barrasford** Nthumb
45	H3	**Barrhead** E Rens
40	D4	**Barrhill** S Ayrs
30	C7	**Barrow upon Soar** Leics
36	E6	**Barrow-in-Furness** Cumb
33	H3	**Barrowford** Lancs
5	K1	**Barry** V Glam
16	C2	**Barton** Cambs
32	E3	**Barton** Lancs
38	C3	**Barton** N York
23	J3	**Barton Seagrave** Nhants
23	L7	**Barton-le-Clay** Beds
29	J7	**Barton-under-Needwood** Staffs
35	G5	**Barton-upon-Humber** N Linc
62	h2	**Barvas** W Isls
22	E2	**Barwell** Leics
16	F7	**Basildon** Essex
9	G1	**Basingstoke** Hants
29	J3	**Baslow** Derbys
42	A8	**Bassenthwaite** Cumb

31 G7 **Baston** Lincs
13 H5 **Bath** BaNES
46 A3 **Bathgate** W Loth
33 L4 **Batley** Kirk
10 F6 **Battle** E Susx
31 H3 **Baumber** Lincs
25 H4 **Bawdeswell** Norfk
17 L4 **Bawdsey** Suffk
34 D7 **Bawtry** Donc
36 F6 **Baycliff** Cumb
28 C8 **Bayston Hill** Shrops
15 G5 **Beaconsfield** Bucks
47 L6 **Beadnell** Nthumb
4 E5 **Beaford** Devon
47 K5 **Beal** Nthumb
7 H2 **Beaminster** Dorset
9 L2 **Beare Green** Surrey
10 F3 **Bearsted** Kent
41 L2 **Beattock** D & G
8 E5 **Beaulieu** Hants
58 D5 **Beauly** Highld
26 E3 **Beaumaris** IOA
7 b2 **Beaumont** Jersey
4 D7 **Beaworthy** Devon
27 L2 **Bebington** Wirral
25 L6 **Beccles** Suffk
24 E7 **Beck Row** Suffk
13 L4 **Beckhampton** Wilts
30 E4 **Beckingham** Lincs
13 H6 **Beckington** Somset
38 C4 **Bedale** N York
26 E5 **Beddgelert** Gwynd
23 K5 **Bedford** Beds
43 K4 **Bedlington** Nthumb
12 C2 **Bedlinog** Myr Td
22 E2 **Bedworth** Warwks
35 H2 **Beeford** E R Yk
29 J3 **Beeley** Derbys
6 F3 **Beer** Devon
28 C4 **Beeston** Ches
30 B6 **Beeston** Notts
41 J5 **Beeswing** D & G
37 H5 **Beetham** Cumb
25 G4 **Beetley** Norfk
20 F3 **Beguildy** Powys
45 G3 **Beith** N Ayrs
47 K6 **Belford** Nthumb
42 F4 **Bellingham** Nthumb
44 A5 **Bellochantuy** Ag & B
45 K2 **Bellshill** N Lans
29 K5 **Belper** Derbys
43 H4 **Belsay** Nthumb
34 E6 **Belton** N Linc
25 L5 **Belton** Norfk
9 G6 **Bembridge** IOW
39 L6 **Bempton** E R Yk
52 F6 **Benderloch** Ag & B
10 F5 **Benenden** Kent
26 D2 **Benllech** IOA
14 D5 **Benson** Oxon
9 H2 **Bentley** Hants
24 B6 **Benwick** Cambs
3 K4 **Bere Alston** Devon
3 K4 **Bere Ferrers** Devon
7 L3 **Bere Regis** Dorset
13 G2 **Berkeley** Gloucs
15 G3 **Berkhamsted** Herts
56 D4 **Bernisdale** Highld
65 G5 **Berriedale** Highld
20 F1 **Berriew** Powys
12 D6 **Berrow** Somset
13 K8 **Berwick St John** Wilts
47 K4 **Berwick-upon-Tweed** Nthumb
11 G4 **Bethersden** Kent
26 E3 **Bethesda** Gwynd
64 D2 **Bettyhill** Highld
27 G4 **Betws-y-coed** Conwy
27 H3 **Betws-yn-Rhos** Conwy
20 D5 **Beulah** Powys
35 G3 **Beverley** E R Yk

21 L3 **Bewdley** Worcs
10 F7 **Bexhill** E Susx
13 L1 **Bibury** Gloucs
14 D2 **Bicester** Oxon
5 H6 **Bickleigh** Devon
11 G4 **Biddenden** Kent
12 E6 **Biddisham** Somset
28 F4 **Biddulph** Staffs
4 D5 **Bideford** Devon
22 C5 **Bidford-on-Avon** Warwks
3 M6 **Bigbury-on-Sea** Devon
46 B6 **Biggar** S Lans
10 C3 **Biggin Hill** Gt Lon
23 M5 **Biggleswade** Beds
17 H3 **Bildeston** Suffk
16 E7 **Billericay** Essex
31 G6 **Billingborough** Lincs
38 E2 **Billingham** S on T
31 H4 **Billinghay** Lincs
9 K3 **Billingshurst** W Susx
31 K3 **Bilsby** Lincs
30 C4 **Bilsthorpe** Notts
35 H7 **Binbrook** Lincs
14 F6 **Binfield** Br For
30 D5 **Bingham** Notts
33 K3 **Bingley** Brad
22 A8 **Birdlip** Gloucs
32 C7 **Birkenhead** Wirral
22 B2 **Birmingham** Birm
30 C8 **Birstall** Leics
43 K6 **Birtley** Gatesd
38 C1 **Bishop Auckland** Dur
13 G5 **Bishop Sutton** BaNES
21 G2 **Bishop's Castle** Shrops
22 A7 **Bishop's Cleeve** Gloucs
21 K5 **Bishop's Frome** Herefs
16 D5 **Bishop's Stortford** Herts
8 F4 **Bishop's Waltham** Hants
12 C7 **Bishops Lydeard** Somset
6 C4 **Bishopsteignton** Devon
19 J7 **Bishopston** Swans
13 M3 **Bishopstone** Swindn
30 F6 **Bitchfield** Lincs
13 G4 **Bitton** S Glos
22 F1 **Blaby** Leics
4 D6 **Black Torrington** Devon
28 E6 **Blackbrook** Staffs
32 F4 **Blackburn** Bl w D
50 E6 **Blackford** P & K
19 M7 **Blackmill** Brdgnd
32 C3 **Blackpool** Bpool
8 F6 **Blackwater** IOW
44 C5 **Blackwaterfoot** N Ayrs
12 C2 **Blackwood** Caerph
45 L4 **Blackwood** S Lans
14 C3 **Bladon** Oxon
26 F5 **Blaenau Ffestiniog** Gwynd
12 D1 **Blaenavon** Torfn
19 L6 **Blaengarw** Brdgnd
18 F2 **Blaenporth** Cerdgn
12 F5 **Blagdon** N Som
54 C7 **Blair Atholl** P & K
51 G3 **Blairgowrie** P & K
49 K5 **Blairmore** Ag & B
13 G1 **Blakeney** Gloucs
23 G5 **Blakesley** Nhants
43 G6 **Blanchland** Nthumb
7 L2 **Blandford Forum** Dorset
50 B8 **Blanefield** Stirlg

34 D6 **Blaxton** Donc
43 J5 **Blaydon** Gatesd
12 F6 **Bleadney** Somset
12 E5 **Bleadon** N Som
11 J3 **Blean** Kent
20 F4 **Bleddfa** Powys
10 B3 **Bletchingley** Surrey
23 J6 **Bletchley** M Keyn
23 K4 **Bletsoe** Beds
14 C5 **Blewbury** Oxon
25 J3 **Blickling** Norfk
30 C4 **Blidworth** Notts
10 C4 **Blindley Heath** Surrey
3 G4 **Blisland** Cnwll
22 E6 **Bloxham** Oxon
38 B7 **Blubberhouses** N York
5 J3 **Blue Anchor** Somset
43 K4 **Blyth** Nthumb
34 E7 **Blyton** Lincs
46 A2 **Bo'ness** Falk
54 D3 **Boat of Garten** Highld
61 H5 **Boddam** Abers
27 J3 **Bodfari** Denbgs
26 C6 **Bodfuan** Gwynd
10 F5 **Bodiam** E Susx
3 G4 **Bodmin** Cnwll
9 J6 **Bognor Regis** W Susx
29 G3 **Bollington** Ches
10 B6 **Bolney** W Susx
29 L3 **Bolsover** Derbys
32 F6 **Bolton** Bolton
33 J2 **Bolton Abbey** N York
37 H6 **Bolton le Sands** Lancs
3 H3 **Bolventor** Cnwll
64 C8 **Bonar Bridge** Highld
42 D1 **Bonchester Bridge** Border
46 D4 **Bonnyrigg** Mdloth
26 D4 **Bontnewydd** Gwynd
12 B4 **Bonvilston** V Glam
36 E3 **Boot** Cumb
36 E4 **Bootle** Cumb
32 C7 **Bootle** Sefton
6 b1 **Bordeaux** Guern
9 H3 **Bordon** Hants
10 E6 **Boreham Street** E Susx
15 J4 **Borehamwood** Herts
10 E3 **Borough Green** Kent
38 D6 **Boroughbridge** N York
29 L6 **Borrowash** Derbys
20 A2 **Borth** Cerdgn
26 E6 **Borth-y-Gest** Gwynd
3 G2 **Boscastle** Cnwll
9 H5 **Bosham** W Susx
18 D6 **Bosherston** Pembks
31 J5 **Boston** Lincs
34 B3 **Boston Spa** Leeds
25 H7 **Botesdale** Suffk
47 M7 **Bothel** Cumb
30 E6 **Bottesford** Leics
10 D4 **Bough Beech** Kent
11 H3 **Boughton Street** Kent
47 M7 **Boulmer** Nthumb
31 G7 **Bourne** Lincs
8 B6 **Bournemouth** Bmouth
21 K2 **Bourton** Shrops
22 C7 **Bourton-on-the-Water** Gloucs
6 B4 **Bovey Tracey** Devon
37 M3 **Bowes** Dur
48 C7 **Bowmore** Ag & B
41 M5 **Bowness-on-Solway** Cumb
13 J4 **Box** Wilts
17 H4 **Boxford** Suffk
23 J4 **Bozeat** Nhants

56 D5 **Bracadale** Highld
23 G6 **Brackley** Nhants
14 F6 **Bracknell** Br For
33 K4 **Bradford** Brad
13 J5 **Bradford-on-Avon** Wilts
8 F6 **Brading** IOW
29 J2 **Bradwell** Derbys
17 H6 **Bradwell-on-Sea** Essex
4 C6 **Bradworthy** Devon
61 b4 **Brae** Shet
54 E5 **Braemar** Abers
65 d2 **Braeswick** Ork
45 L3 **Braidwood** S Lans
29 J5 **Brailsford** Derbys
16 F5 **Braintree** Essex
36 F2 **Braithwaite** Cumb
8 F3 **Bramdean** Hants
25 K7 **Bramfield** Suffk
34 B3 **Bramham** Leeds
33 L3 **Bramhope** Leeds
14 D7 **Bramley** Hants
9 K2 **Bramley** Surrey
23 M3 **Brampton** Cambs
42 D5 **Brampton** Cumb
8 D4 **Bramshaw** Hants
24 E2 **Brancaster** Norfk
35 H3 **Brandesburton** E R Yk
43 J7 **Brandon** Dur
24 E6 **Brandon** Suffk
22 E3 **Brandon** Warwks
6 E3 **Branscombe** Devon
8 C6 **Bransgore** Hants
30 F3 **Branston** Lincs
36 D2 **Branthwaite** Cumb
29 J4 **Brassington** Derbys
10 D3 **Brasted** Kent
13 J6 **Bratton** Wilts
3 K2 **Bratton Clovelly** Devon
4 F4 **Bratton Fleming** Devon
16 C5 **Braughing** Herts
4 E4 **Braunton** Devon
4 E4 **Brayford** Devon
62 g3 **Breascleit** W Isls
62 g3 **Breasclete** W Isls
19 H4 **Brechfa** Carmth
55 J7 **Brechin** Angus
20 E7 **Brecon** Powys
11 G6 **Brede** E Susx
21 K5 **Bredenbury** Herefs
10 F3 **Bredhurst** Kent
22 A6 **Bredon** Worcs
21 G6 **Bredwardine** Herefs
5 G3 **Brendon** Devon
12 E6 **Brent Knoll** Somset
16 E7 **Brentwood** Essex
11 H5 **Brenzett** Kent
28 E4 **Brereton Green** Ches
28 F8 **Brewood** Staffs
36 C1 **Bride** IOM
3 L2 **Bridestowe** Devon
11 J3 **Bridge** Kent
50 D6 **Bridge of Allan** Stirlg
51 G2 **Bridge of Cally** P & K
51 G5 **Bridge of Earn** P & K
53 K6 **Bridge of Orchy** Ag & B
49 M6 **Bridge of Weir** Rens
48 C6 **Bridgend** Ag & B
19 L7 **Bridgend** Brdgnd
21 L2 **Bridgnorth** Shrops
12 D7 **Bridgwater** Somset
39 L6 **Bridlington** E R Yk
7 H3 **Bridport** Dorset
33 H3 **Brierfield** Lancs
35 G6 **Brigg** N Linc
41 L8 **Brigham** Cumb
33 K4 **Brighouse** Calder

8 E7 **Brighstone** IOW
17 J5 **Brightlingsea** Essex
10 B7 **Brighton** Br & H
23 K2 **Brigstock** Nhants
22 E3 **Brinklow** Warwks
13 K3 **Brinkworth** Wilts
65 c3 **Brinyan** Ork
13 G4 **Bristol** Bristl
6 C6 **Brixham** Torbay
3 L5 **Brixton** Devon
23 H3 **Brixworth** Nhants
13 L3 **Broad Blunsdon** Swindn
13 K8 **Broad Chalke** Wilts
18 C5 **Broad Haven** Pembks
6 D3 **Broadclyst** Devon
56 F6 **Broadford** Highld
11 L2 **Broadstairs** Kent
22 C6 **Broadway** Worcs
7 G2 **Broadwindsor** Dorset
25 J7 **Brockdish** Norfk
8 D5 **Brockenhurst** Hants
17 J1 **Brockford Street** Suffk
21 M8 **Brockworth** Gloucs
44 D4 **Brodick** N Ayrs
25 H7 **Brome** Suffk
21 J3 **Bromfield** Shrops
23 K5 **Bromham** Beds
10 C2 **Bromley** Gt Lon
39 J5 **Brompton** N York
5 H4 **Brompton Regis** Somset
22 A3 **Bromsgrove** Worcs
21 K5 **Bromyard** Herefs
20 F6 **Bronllys** Powys
25 K6 **Brooke** Norfk
11 H5 **Brookland** Kent
15 J4 **Brookmans Park** Herts
43 K2 **Broomhill** Nthumb
64 F7 **Brora** Highld
21 K1 **Broseley** Shrops
34 B4 **Brotherton** N York
39 G2 **Brotton** R & Cl
37 K2 **Brough** Cumb
46 B6 **Broughton** Border
34 F6 **Broughton** N Linc
13 M2 **Broughton Poggs** Oxon
36 F5 **Broughton-in-Furness** Cumb
29 H8 **Brownhills** Wsall
46 B3 **Broxburn** W Loth
16 D5 **Broxted** Essex
25 K5 **Brundall** Norfk
13 G7 **Bruton** Somset
19 K5 **Brynaman** Carmth
20 A1 **Bryncrug** Gwynd
12 C1 **Brynmawr** Blae G
34 D3 **Bubwith** E R Yk
50 B7 **Buchlyvie** Stirlg
23 M4 **Buckden** Cambs
37 M5 **Buckden** N York
6 B5 **Buckfastleigh** Devon
51 H6 **Buckhaven** Fife
13 H8 **Buckhorn Weston** Dorset
60 B3 **Buckie** Moray
23 G6 **Buckingham** Bucks
16 C4 **Buckland** Herts
8 E5 **Bucklers Hard** Hants
27 L4 **Buckley** Flints
28 E2 **Bucklow Hill** Ches
30 E7 **Buckminster** Leics
4 B6 **Bude** Cnwll
6 D4 **Budleigh Salterton** Devon
2 F5 **Bugle** Cnwll
20 E5 **Builth Wells** Powys
8 C2 **Bulford** Wilts
22 E2 **Bulkington** Warwks

16 E8 **Bulphan** Thurr
23 K2 **Bulwick** Nhants
48 C2 **Bunessan** Ag & B
25 K6 **Bungay** Suffk
30 C6 **Bunny** Notts
16 C4 **Buntingford** Herts
25 H6 **Bunwell Street** Norfk
13 M5 **Burbage** Wilts
17 G4 **Bures** Essex
13 M1 **Burford** Oxon
10 B6 **Burgess Hill** W Susx
42 B6 **Burgh by Sands** Cumb
25 L5 **Burgh Castle** Norfk
31 K4 **Burgh le Marsh** Lincs
59 J3 **Burghead** Moray
14 D6 **Burghfield** W Berk
8 C5 **Burley** Hants
33 K3 **Burley in Wharfedale** Brad
28 D5 **Burleydam** Ches
28 C7 **Burlton** Shrops
38 C5 **Burneston** N York
24 F2 **Burnham Market** Norfk
24 F2 **Burnham Overy Staithe** Norfk
17 H7 **Burnham-on-Crouch** Essex
12 D6 **Burnham-on-Sea** Somset
33 G4 **Burnley** Lancs
43 J6 **Burnopfield** Dur
46 C2 **Burntisland** Fife
61 d3 **Burravoe** Shet
51 G3 **Burrelton** P & K
4 F5 **Burrington** Devon
19 H6 **Burry Port** Carmth
32 D5 **Burscough Bridge** Lancs
8 E5 **Bursledon** Hants
27 L3 **Burton** Ches
39 K6 **Burton Agnes** E R Yk
7 H3 **Burton Bradstock** Dorset
39 K6 **Burton Fleming** E R Yk
30 C5 **Burton Joyce** Notts
23 J3 **Burton Latimer** Nhants
34 F5 **Burton upon Stather** N Linc
29 J7 **Burton upon Trent** Staffs
37 H5 **Burton-in-Kendal** Cumb
10 E5 **Burwash** E Susx
16 E1 **Burwell** Cambs
65 c6 **Burwick** Ork
33 G5 **Bury** Bury
17 G2 **Bury St Edmunds** Suffk
15 H4 **Bushey** Herts
17 L3 **Butley** Suffk
36 E2 **Buttermere** Cumb
31 J5 **Butterwick** Lincs
27 K8 **Buttington** Powys
10 D6 **Buxted** E Susx
29 H3 **Buxton** Derbys
12 F6 **Bwlch** Powys
15 H7 **Byfleet** Surrey
27 H4 **Bylchau** Conwy
42 F2 **Byness** Nthumb

C

2 D8 **Cadgwith** Cnwll
12 E3 **Caerleon** Newpt
26 D4 **Caernarfon** Gwynd
12 C3 **Caerphilly** Caerph

20 E2 **Caersws** Powys
12 F3 **Caerwent** Mons
27 J3 **Caerwys** Flints
49 K3 **Cairndow** Ag & B
40 B5 **Cairnryan** D & G
25 L5 **Caister-on-Sea** Norfk
35 H6 **Caistor** Lincs
25 J5 **Caistor St Edmund** Norfk
42 B7 **Caldbeck** Cumb
23 J2 **Caldecott** Rutlnd
36 D3 **Calder Bridge** Cumb
45 L2 **Caldercruix** N Lans
12 F3 **Caldicot** Mons
65 d2 **Calfsound** Ork
52 B5 **Calgary** Ag & B
50 B6 **Callander** Stirlg
3 J4 **Callington** Cnwll
13 K4 **Calne** Wilts
8 E5 **Calshot** Hants
54 C7 **Calvine** P & K
11 H6 **Camber** E Susx
14 F7 **Camberley** Surrey
43 H4 **Cambo** Nthumb
2 C6 **Camborne** Cnwll
16 B2 **Cambourne** Cambs
16 C2 **Cambridge** Cambs
13 H2 **Cambridge** Gloucs
45 K2 **Cambuslang** S Lans
15 K5 **Camden Town** Gt Lon
3 G3 **Camelford** Cnwll
44 B5 **Campbeltown** Ag & B
31 K3 **Candlesby** Lincs
58 C6 **Cannich** Highld
12 D7 **Cannington** Somset
29 G8 **Cannock** Staffs
42 C4 **Canonbie** D & G
11 J3 **Canterbury** Kent
16 F8 **Canvey Island** Essex
48 b2 **Caoles** Ag & B
9 L2 **Capel** Surrey
20 B3 **Capel Bangor** Cerdgn
26 F4 **Capel Curig** Conwy
17 J4 **Capel St Mary** Suffk
50 F3 **Caputh** P & K
30 D5 **Car Colston** Notts
56 D6 **Carbost** Highld
12 C4 **Cardiff** Cardif
18 E2 **Cardigan** Cerdgn
23 L5 **Cardington** Beds
49 L5 **Cardross** Ag & B
18 D6 **Carew** Pembks
46 F4 **Carfraemill** Border
5 J3 **Carhampton** Somset
37 G5 **Cark** Cumb
62 g3 **Carlabhagh** W Isls
42 C6 **Carlisle** Cumb
46 C4 **Carlops** Border
62 g3 **Carloway** W Isls
38 A5 **Carlton** N York
34 D4 **Carlton** N York
30 E4 **Carlton-on-Trent** Notts
45 L3 **Carluke** S Lans
19 G4 **Carmarthen** Carmth
39 K6 **Carnaby** E R Yk
37 H6 **Carnforth** Lancs
20 D2 **Carno** Powys
2 E6 **Carnon Downs** Cnwll
51 K4 **Carnoustie** Angus
46 A5 **Carnwath** S Lans
44 C4 **Carradale** Ag & B
59 H6 **Carrbridge** Highld
7 b1 **Carrefour** Jersey
49 K4 **Carrick Castle** Ag & B
41 J3 **Carronbridge** D & G
41 L5 **Carrutherstown** D & G
40 F3 **Carsphairn** D & G
45 M3 **Carstairs** S Lans
14 A3 **Carterton** Oxon
37 G5 **Cartmel** Cumb

37 J5 **Casterton** Lancs
24 F4 **Castle Acre** Norfk
42 D6 **Castle Carrock** Cumb
13 G7 **Castle Cary** Somset
29 L6 **Castle Donington** Leics
41 H5 **Castle Douglas** D & G
16 F4 **Castle Hedingham** Essex
24 D4 **Castle Rising** Norfk
62 b14 **Castlebay** W Isls
34 B4 **Castleford** Wakefd
18 C6 **Castlemartin** Pembks
43 H6 **Castleside** Dur
29 H2 **Castleton** Derbys
39 G3 **Castleton** N York
12 D3 **Castleton** Newpt
65 H2 **Castletown** Highld
36 b4 **Castletown** IOM
6 a2 **Catel** Guern
10 C3 **Caterham** Surrey
25 K4 **Catfield** Norfk
37 H6 **Caton** Lancs
45 J5 **Catrine** E Ayrs
10 F6 **Catsfield** E Susx
38 C4 **Catterick** N York
30 D4 **Caunton** Notts
59 G4 **Cawdor** Highld
3 K5 **Cawsand** Cnwll
16 B2 **Caxton** Cambs
30 F5 **Caythorpe** Lincs
39 K5 **Cayton** N York
26 C1 **Cemaes** IOA
20 C1 **Cemmaes Road** Powys
51 J5 **Ceres** Fife
7 J2 **Cerne Abbas** Dorset
27 H5 **Cerrigydrudion** Conwy
33 H6 **Chadderton** Oldham
14 B2 **Chadlington** Oxon
6 A3 **Chagford** Devon
8 E7 **Chale** IOW
15 G4 **Chalfont St Giles** Bucks
15 G5 **Chalfont St Peter** Bucks
13 J2 **Chalford** Gloucs
4 F3 **Challacombe** Devon
11 H3 **Challock** Kent
8 E4 **Chandler's Ford** Hants
31 L3 **Chapel St Leonards** Lincs
29 H2 **Chapel-en-le-Frith** Derbys
34 A6 **Chapeltown** Sheff
13 J6 **Chapmanslade** Wilts
6 F2 **Chard** Somset
11 H4 **Charing** Kent
14 B2 **Charlbury** Oxon
22 D5 **Charlecote** Warwks
22 A7 **Charlton Kings** Gloucs
7 L2 **Charlton Marshall** Dorset
10 B4 **Charlwood** Surrey
7 G3 **Charmouth** Dorset
11 J3 **Chartham** Kent
33 G3 **Chatburn** Lancs
10 F2 **Chatham** Medway
24 B7 **Chatteris** Cambs
47 K6 **Chatton** Nthumb
6 F6 **Chawleigh** Devon
9 G3 **Chawton** Hants
29 G5 **Cheadle** Staffs
33 H7 **Cheadle** Stockp
12 F6 **Cheddar** Somset
29 G5 **Cheddleton** Staffs
28 F3 **Chelford** Ches
16 F6 **Chelmsford** Essex
22 A7 **Cheltenham** Gloucs

12 F3 **Chepstow** Mons
8 F3 **Cheriton** Hants
5 H6 **Cheriton Fitzpaine** Devon
15 G6 **Chertsey** Surrey
15 G4 **Chesham** Bucks
15 K4 **Cheshunt** Herts
28 B3 **Chester** Ches
43 K6 **Chester-le-Street** Dur
29 K3 **Chesterfield** Derbys
13 G5 **Chew Magna** BaNES
13 G6 **Chewton Mendip** Somset
23 J5 **Chicheley** M Keyn
9 H5 **Chichester** W Susx
7 J4 **Chickerell** Dorset
13 J7 **Chicklade** Wilts
9 J3 **Chiddingfold** Surrey
14 C6 **Chieveley** W Berk
16 C7 **Chigwell** Essex
28 B3 **Childer Thornton** Ches
11 J3 **Chilham** Kent
47 K7 **Chillingham** Nthumb
6 B7 **Chillington** Devon
13 K7 **Chilmark** Wilts
4 C6 **Chilsworthy** Devon
14 A6 **Chilton Foliat** Wilts
14 E4 **Chinnor** Oxon
16 E1 **Chippenham** Cambs
13 J4 **Chippenham** Wilts
15 G4 **Chipperfield** Herts
32 F3 **Chipping** Lancs
22 C6 **Chipping Campden** Gloucs
22 D7 **Chipping Norton** Oxon
16 D6 **Chipping Ongar** Essex
13 H3 **Chipping Sodbury** S Glos
22 F5 **Chipping Warden** Nhants
21 G1 **Chirbury** Shrops
27 L6 **Chirk** Wrexhm
47 J4 **Chirnside** Border
13 M4 **Chiseldon** Swindn
13 K6 **Chitterne** Wilts
4 F5 **Chittlehampton** Devon
15 G7 **Chobham** Surrey
8 C2 **Cholderton** Wilts
32 E5 **Chorley** Lancs
15 G4 **Chorleywood** Herts
8 C6 **Christchurch** Dorset
6 C4 **Chudleigh** Devon
6 C4 **Chudleigh Knighton** Devon
4 F6 **Chulmleigh** Devon
21 H2 **Church Stretton** Shrops
14 A2 **Churchill** Oxon
21 G2 **Churchstoke** Powys
6 C6 **Churston Ferrers** Torbay
9 H3 **Churt** Surrey
21 K8 **Cinderford** Gloucs
13 K2 **Cirencester** Gloucs
44 B3 **Clachan** Ag & B
50 E7 **Clackmannan** Clacks
17 J5 **Clacton-on-Sea** Essex
14 A4 **Clanfield** Oxon
44 C3 **Claonaig** Ag & B
23 K5 **Clapham** Beds
37 K6 **Clapham** N York
16 F3 **Clare** Suffk
62 F5 **Clashnessie** Highld
60 C6 **Clatt** Abers
22 C4 **Claverdon** Warwks
16 D4 **Clavering** Essex
4 C7 **Clawton** Devon
29 K4 **Clay Cross** Derbys
17 J3 **Claydon** Suffk

36 D2 **Cleator Moor** Cumb
35 J6 **Cleethorpes** NE Lin
12 F5 **Cleeve** N Som
22 B7 **Cleeve Hill** Gloucs
21 K3 **Cleobury Mortimer** Shrops
21 K2 **Cleobury North** Shrops
12 E4 **Clevedon** N Som
32 C3 **Cleveleys** Lancs
25 G2 **Cley next the Sea** Norfk
10 F2 **Cliffe** Medway
34 D4 **Cliffe** N York
10 F2 **Cliffe Woods** Medway
37 H2 **Clifton** Cumb
21 L4 **Clifton upon Teme** Worcs
9 K5 **Climping** W Susx
33 G3 **Clitheroe** Lancs
61 G5 **Clola** Abers
23 L6 **Clophill** Beds
7 H2 **Closworth** Somset
39 J4 **Cloughton** N York
55 G6 **Clova** Angus
4 C5 **Clovelly** Devon
46 E6 **Clovenfords** Border
30 B3 **Clowne** Derbys
21 L3 **Clows Top** Worcs
21 G3 **Clun** Shrops
19 J6 **Clydach** Swans
45 H2 **Clydebank** W Duns
49 K5 **Clynder** Ag & B
26 D5 **Clynnog-fawr** Gwynd
20 F6 **Clyro** Powys
6 D3 **Clyst St Mary** Devon
21 K1 **Coalport** Wrekin
29 L7 **Coalville** Leics
45 K2 **Coatbridge** N Lans
10 E2 **Cobham** Kent
47 H3 **Cockburnspath** Border
41 L8 **Cockermouth** Cumb
9 J4 **Cocking** W Susx
17 J2 **Coddenham** Suffk
13 K7 **Codford St Mary** Wilts
15 J3 **Codicote** Herts
29 L5 **Codnor** Derbys
21 M1 **Codsall** Staffs
27 L5 **Coedpoeth** Wrexhm
17 G5 **Coggeshall** Essex
17 H5 **Colchester** Essex
14 C6 **Cold Ash** W Berk
23 G3 **Cold Ashby** Nhants
13 H4 **Cold Ashton** S Glos
17 G7 **Cold Norton** Essex
47 J3 **Coldingham** Border
47 H5 **Coldstream** Border
13 G1 **Coleford** Gloucs
13 J4 **Colerne** Wilts
22 C2 **Coleshill** Warwks
49 J6 **Colintraive** Ag & B
15 K2 **Collier's End** Herts
61 G6 **Collieston** Abers
13 M6 **Collingbourne Ducis** Wilts
34 B3 **Collingham** Leeds
40 C3 **Colmonell** S Ayrs
13 L2 **Coln St Aldwyns** Gloucs
33 H3 **Colne** Lancs
17 G4 **Colne Engaine** Essex
60 D6 **Colpy** Abers
30 F7 **Colsterworth** Lincs
25 J4 **Coltishall** Norfk
43 G4 **Colwell** Nthumb
27 G2 **Colwyn Bay** Conwy
6 F3 **Colyford** Devon
6 F3 **Colyton** Devon
4 E3 **Combe Martin** Devon
9 J2 **Compton** Surrey

14 C5 **Compton** W Berk
50 D5 **Comrie** P & K
28 F4 **Congleton** Ches
12 E5 **Congresbury** N Som
31 H4 **Coningsby** Lincs
23 M2 **Conington** Cambs
34 C6 **Conisbrough** Donc
36 F4 **Coniston** Cumb
27 L3 **Connah's Quay** Flints
52 F7 **Connel** Ag & B
58 E4 **Conon Bridge** Highld
43 H6 **Consett** Dur
2 D7 **Constantine** Cnwll
58 D4 **Contin** Highld
17 G3 **Conwy** Conwy
14 F5 **Cookham** W & M
9 L4 **Coolham** W Susx
8 B3 **Coombe Bissett** Wilts
21 M7 **Coombe Hill** Gloucs
17 J3 **Copdock** Suffk
17 G5 **Copford Green** Essex
38 B2 **Copley** Dur
5 G6 **Copplestone** Devon
10 B4 **Copthorne** W Susx
7 a2 **Corbiere** Jersey
43 G5 **Corbridge** Nthumb
23 J2 **Corby** Nhants
30 F7 **Corby Glen** Lincs
6 F1 **Corfe** Somset
7 M4 **Corfe Castle** Dorset
55 G4 **Corgarff** Abers
47 H5 **Cornhill-on-Tweed** Nthumb
3 L5 **Cornwood** Devon
53 H3 **Corpach** Highld
44 D4 **Corrie** N Ayrs
26 F8 **Corris** Gwynd
13 J4 **Corsham** Wilts
13 J3 **Corston** Wilts
25 M6 **Corton** Suffk
27 J5 **Corwen** Denbgs
16 F8 **Coryton** Thurr
22 F2 **Cosby** Leics
28 C4 **Cotebrook** Ches
38 A2 **Cotherstone** Dur
16 C1 **Cottenham** Cambs
16 B4 **Cottered** Herts
35 G4 **Cottingham** E R Yk
49 K5 **Coulport** Ag & B
46 B6 **Coulter** S Lans
23 G2 **Countesthorpe** Leics
51 G3 **Coupar Angus** P & K
62 B8 **Cove** Highld
22 E3 **Coventry** Covtry
2 D8 **Coverack** Cnwll
31 H7 **Cowbit** Lincs
12 B4 **Cowbridge** V Glam
10 D4 **Cowden** Kent
51 G7 **Cowdenbeath** Fife
8 E6 **Cowes** IOW
9 L4 **Cowfold** W Susx
33 J3 **Cowling** N York
10 F3 **Coxheath** Kent
38 E5 **Coxwold** N York
45 H6 **Coylton** S Ayrs
54 D3 **Coylumbridge** Highld
4 B7 **Crackington Haven** Cnwll
37 M7 **Cracoe** N York
3 J5 **Crafthole** Cnwll
59 L5 **Craigellachie** Moray
48 D6 **Craighouse** Ag & B
52 E6 **Craignure** Ag & B
51 J5 **Craigrothie** Fife
51 L6 **Crail** Fife
47 G7 **Crailing** Border
43 K4 **Cramlington** Nthumb
8 B4 **Cranborne** Dorset
10 F3 **Cranbrook** Kent
23 K6 **Cranfield** Beds
21 M8 **Cranham** Gloucs
9 K2 **Cranleigh** Surrey

47 G4 **Cranshaws** Border
49 H4 **Crarae** Ag & B
47 M7 **Craster** Nthumb
54 F5 **Crathie** Abers
38 E3 **Crathorne** N York
21 H3 **Craven Arms** Shrops
46 A7 **Crawford** S Lans
45 M5 **Crawfordjohn** S Lans
10 B5 **Crawley** W Susx
10 C4 **Crawley Down** W Susx
62 c10 **Creagorry** W Isls
21 H6 **Credenhill** Herefs
5 G7 **Crediton** Devon
40 F6 **Creetown** D & G
36 a4 **Cregneash** IOM
21 K1 **Cressage** Shrops
28 E4 **Crewe** Ches
7 G2 **Crewkerne** Somset
53 K7 **Crianlarich** Stirlg
26 D6 **Criccieth** Gwynd
20 F7 **Crickhowell** Powys
13 L3 **Cricklade** Wilts
50 D5 **Crieff** P & K
61 H4 **Crimond** Abers
49 G4 **Crinan** Ag & B
25 J5 **Cringleford** Norfk
6 B3 **Crockernwell** Devon
41 J4 **Crocketford** D & G
42 D6 **Croglin** Cumb
59 G3 **Cromarty** Highld
59 G3 **Cromdale** Highld
25 J2 **Cromer** Norfk
29 K4 **Cromford** Derbys
30 E4 **Cromwell** Notts
43 J7 **Crook** Dur
37 H5 **Crooklands** Cumb
22 F5 **Cropredy** Oxon
39 G4 **Cropton** N York
36 b3 **Crosby** IOM
32 C6 **Crosby** Sefton
19 H5 **Cross Hands** Carmth
10 D6 **Cross in Hand** E Susx
46 B2 **Crossford** Fife
45 L3 **Crossford** S Lans
45 G6 **Crosshill** S Ayrs
12 D3 **Crosskeys** Caerph
41 H5 **Crossmichael** D & G
21 M4 **Crossway Green** Worcs
37 G4 **Crosthwaite** Cumb
10 D5 **Crowborough** E Susx
5 K4 **Crowcombe** Somset
10 F6 **Crowhurst** E Susx
31 H8 **Crowland** Lincs
34 E5 **Crowle** N Linc
14 F7 **Crowthorne** Wokham
30 E6 **Croxton Kerrial** Leics
59 G4 **Croy** Highld
4 D4 **Croyde** Devon
15 K7 **Croydon** Gt Lon
61 H5 **Cruden Bay** Abers
28 D7 **Crudgington** Wrekin
13 K3 **Crudwell** Wilts
19 K5 **Crynant** Neath
10 B5 **Cuckfield** W Susx
30 C3 **Cuckney** Notts
28 D3 **Cuddington** Ches
34 B6 **Cudworth** Barns
15 K4 **Cuffley** Herts
37 J1 **Culgaith** Cumb
60 C3 **Cullen** Moray
5 J6 **Cullompton** Devon
5 K6 **Culmstock** Devon
45 L1 **Cumbernauld** N Lans
60 E4 **Cuminestown** Abers
41 L5 **Cummertrees** D & G
45 J5 **Cumnock** E Ayrs
14 C4 **Cumnor** Oxon
42 D6 **Cumrew** Cumb
51 J5 **Cupar** Fife
12 E8 **Curry Rivel** Somset

12 D2 **Cwmbran** Torfn
20 C3 **Cwmystwyth** Cerdgn
19 L6 **Cymer** Neath
19 G4 **Cynwyl Elfed** Carmth

D

40 D2 **Dailly** S Ayrs
51 J5 **Dairsie** Fife
41 J5 **Dalbeattie** D & G
36 a3 **Dalby** IOM
18 B5 **Dale** Pembks
46 C2 **Dalgety Bay** Fife
64 E3 **Dalhalvaig** Highld
46 D3 **Dalkeith** Mdloth
59 J4 **Dallas** Moray
53 J7 **Dalmally** Ag & B
45 H7 **Dalmellington** E Ayrs
45 G3 **Dalry** N Ayrs
45 G6 **Dalrymple** E Ayrs
42 B6 **Dalston** Cumb
41 L4 **Dalton** D & G
36 F6 **Dalton-in-Furness**
Cumb
54 A5 **Dalwhinnie** Highld
8 B4 **Damerham** Hants
16 F6 **Danbury** Essex
38 C2 **Darlington** Darltn
43 J5 **Darras Hall** Nthumb
34 B5 **Darrington** Wakefd
17 L1 **Darsham** Suffk
10 D2 **Dartford** Kent
6 B5 **Dartington** Devon
6 C6 **Dartmouth** Devon
45 J4 **Darvel** E Ayrs
32 F5 **Darwen** Bl w D
15 G6 **Datchet** W & M
59 H5 **Dava** Highld
28 D3 **Davenham** Ches
23 G4 **Daventry** Nhants
58 F5 **Daviot** Highld
6 C4 **Dawlish** Devon
11 L3 **Deal** Kent
41 L7 **Dearham** Cumb
17 J2 **Debenham** Suffk
22 F6 **Deddington** Oxon
17 H4 **Dedham** Essex
31 H8 **Deeping St James**
Lincs
31 H7 **Deeping St Nicholas**
Lincs
27 G7 **Deganwy** Conwy
3 G3 **Delabole** Cnwll
27 J3 **Denbigh** Denbgs
33 L6 **Denby Dale** Kirk
15 G5 **Denham** Bucks
46 F7 **Denholm** Border
9 G5 **Denmead** Hants
17 K1 **Dennington** Suffk
50 D8 **Denny** Falk
11 K4 **Densole** Kent
37 K5 **Dent** Cumb
33 H7 **Denton** Tamesd
29 K6 **Derby** C Derb
36 b4 **Derbyhaven** IOM
25 G4 **Dereham** Norfk
24 E3 **Dersingham** Norfk
52 B5 **Dervaig** Ag & B
23 H3 **Desborough** Nhants
22 F1 **Desford** Leics
20 B3 **Devil's Bridge** Cerdgn
13 K5 **Devizes** Wilts
33 L5 **Dewsbury** Kirk
9 L4 **Dial Post** W Susx
14 C5 **Didcot** Oxon
13 J3 **Didmarton** Gloucs
31 G4 **Digby** Lincs
21 H5 **Dilwyn** Herefs
27 G7 **Dinas-Mawddwy**
Gwynd

58 E4 **Dingwall** Highld
30 B2 **Dinnington** Rothm
44 C4 **Dippen** Ag & B
29 L7 **Diseworth** Leics
38 D6 **Dishforth** N York
29 G2 **Disley** Ches
25 H7 **Diss** Norfk
10 B6 **Ditchling** E Susx
6 C6 **Dittisham** Devon
21 K2 **Ditton Priors** Shrops
3 H4 **Dobwalls** Cnwll
24 E3 **Docking** Norfk
24 B6 **Doddington** Cambs
11 G3 **Doddington** Kent
47 K6 **Doddington** Nthumb
33 L6 **Dodworth** Barns
26 F7 **Dolgellau** Gwynd
50 E6 **Dollar** Clacks
46 B5 **Dolphinton** S Lans
4 E6 **Dolton** Devon
26 F5 **Dolwyddelan** Conwy
34 C6 **Doncaster** Donc
31 H6 **Donington** Lincs
7 K3 **Dorchester** Dorset
14 D4 **Dorchester** Oxon
22 D1 **Dordon** Warwks
58 E5 **Dores** Highld
9 L2 **Dorking** Surrey
57 H6 **Dornie** Highld
59 G1 **Dornoch** Highld
21 J1 **Dorrington** Shrops
21 G6 **Dorstone** Herefs
36 c3 **Douglas** IOM
45 L5 **Douglas** S Lans
65 b3 **Doonby** Ork
50 C6 **Doune** Stirlg
3 L4 **Dousland** Devon
11 L4 **Dover** Kent
29 H6 **Doveridge** Derbys
50 E3 **Dowally** P & K
3 J5 **Downderry** Cnwll
24 D5 **Downham Market**
Norfk
8 C4 **Downton** Wilts
22 A5 **Drakes Broughton**
Worcs
12 F6 **Draycott** Somset
25 J4 **Drayton** Norfk
14 C4 **Drayton** Oxon
39 J7 **Driffield** E R Yk
52 C5 **Drimnin** Highld
22 A4 **Droitwich** Worcs
29 K3 **Dronfield** Derbys
8 F4 **Droxford** Hants
63 G4 **Drumbeg** Highld
55 L6 **Drumlithie** Abers
40 C7 **Drummore** D & G
58 D6 **Drumnadrochit**
Highld
50 A7 **Drymen** Stirlg
56 D2 **Drynoch** Highld
23 K1 **Duddington** Nhants
22 A2 **Dudley** Dudley
29 K5 **Duffield** Derbys
59 L5 **Dufftown** Moray
59 K3 **Duffus** Moray
57 G6 **Duirinish** Highld
59 H6 **Dulnain Bridge**
Highld
5 H4 **Dulverton** Somset
49 M5 **Dumbarton** W Duns
41 K4 **Dumfries** D & G
47 G2 **Dunbar** E Loth
65 H5 **Dunbeath** Highld
50 D8 **Dunblane** Stirlg
22 F3 **Dunchurch** Warwks
51 J4 **Dundee** C Dund
45 G4 **Dundonald** S Ayrs
57 K1 **Dundonnell** Highld
41 H6 **Dundrennan** D & G
46 B2 **Dunfermline** Fife
50 F3 **Dunkeld** P & K

45 H3 **Dunlop** E Ayrs
65 H2 **Dunnet** Highld
50 F5 **Dunning** P & K
49 K5 **Dunoon** Ag & B
40 C6 **Dunragit** D & G
47 H4 **Duns** Border
41 J4 **Dunscore** D & G
9 K3 **Dunsfold** Surrey
6 B3 **Dunsford** Devon
32 F2 **Dunsop Bridge** Lancs
15 G2 **Dunstable** Beds
5 J3 **Dunster** Somset
7 K2 **Duntish** Dorset
44 F6 **Dunure** S Ayrs
19 J6 **Dunvant** Swans
56 C4 **Dunvegan** Highld
25 L8 **Dunwich** Suffk
43 K7 **Durham** Dur
63 J2 **Durness** Highld
53 G5 **Duror** Highld
8 C2 **Durrington** Wilts
55 L5 **Durris** Abers
13 H2 **Dursley** Gloucs
16 D3 **Duxford** Cambs
55 M3 **Dyce** C Aber
26 E7 **Dyffryn Ardudwy**
Gwynd
59 H4 **Dyke** Moray
11 J5 **Dymchurch** Kent
21 K7 **Dymock** Gloucs

E

42 A4 **Eaglesfield** D & G
45 J3 **Eaglesham** E Rens
15 J5 **Ealing** Gt Lon
33 H3 **Earby** Lancs
21 G5 **Eardisley** Herefs
24 B7 **Earith** Cambs
14 E6 **Earley** Wokham
23 J4 **Earls Barton** Nhants
17 G4 **Earls Colne** Essex
46 F6 **Earlston** Border
25 K6 **Earsham** Norfk
48 F2 **Easdale** Ag & B
9 J4 **Easebourne** W Susx
43 L7 **Easington** Dur
35 K5 **Easington** E R Yk
38 E6 **Easingwold** N York
39 J5 **East Ayton** N York
31 H2 **East Barkwith** Lincs
17 J4 **East Bergholt** Suffk
7 H1 **East Chinnock**
Somset
8 E6 **East Cowes** IOW
10 D8 **East Dean** E Susx
9 J4 **East Dean** W Susx
30 C7 **East Goscote** Leics
10 C4 **East Grinstead**
W Susx
25 G6 **East Harling** Norfk
10 D6 **East Hoathly** E Susx
15 H8 **East Horsley** Surrey
14 C5 **East Ilsley** W Berk
45 J3 **East Kilbride** S Lans
13 J7 **East Knoyle** Wilts
9 H5 **East Lavant** W Susx
46 F3 **East Linton** E Loth
7 L4 **East Lulworth** Dorset
6 B7 **East Prawle** Devon
9 K5 **East Preston** W Susx
24 F3 **East Rudham** Norfk
46 E3 **East Saltoun** E Loth
30 D5 **East Stoke** Notts
9 H6 **East Wittering**
W Susx
38 B5 **East Witton** N York
10 E7 **Eastbourne** E Susx
11 H2 **Eastchurch** Kent
8 E4 **Eastleigh** Hants

17 K2 **Easton** Suffk
42 A5 **Eastriggs** D & G
11 K3 **Eastry** Kent
29 L5 **Eastwood** Notts
23 L4 **Eaton Socon** Cambs
12 C1 **Ebbw Vale** Blae G
43 H6 **Ebchester** Dur
41 M4 **Ecclefechan** D & G
47 H5 **Eccles** Border
28 F6 **Eccleshall** Staffs
55 K4 **Echt** Abers
29 L2 **Eckington** Derbys
22 A6 **Eckington** Worcs
58 F2 **Edderton** Highld
46 C5 **Eddleston** Border
10 C4 **Edenbridge** Kent
56 D4 **Edinbane** Highld
46 C3 **Edinburgh** C Edin
31 H3 **Edlington** Lincs
43 H6 **Edmundbyers** Dur
47 G6 **Ednam** Border
30 C3 **Edwinstowe** Notts
55 J7 **Edzell** Angus
15 H7 **Effingham** Surrey
4 F6 **Eggesford** Devon
37 M2 **Eggleston** Dur
15 G6 **Egham** Surrey
47 K7 **Eglingham** Nthumb
18 E3 **Eglwyswrw** Pembks
36 D3 **Egremont** Cumb
39 H3 **Egton** N York
39 H3 **Egton Bridge** N York
20 D4 **Elan Village** Powys
59 K3 **Elgin** Moray
56 E7 **Elgol** Highld
11 J4 **Elham** Kent
51 K6 **Elie** Fife
30 D3 **Elkesley** Notts
13 K1 **Elkstone** Gloucs
33 K5 **Elland** Calder
28 B6 **Ellesmere** Shrops
28 B3 **Ellesmere Port** Ches
25 K6 **Ellingham** Norfk
61 G6 **Ellon** Abers
34 F4 **Elloughton** E R Yk
17 H5 **Elmstead Market**
Essex
43 G3 **Elsdon** Nthumb
46 B5 **Elsrickle** S Lans
9 J2 **Elstead** Surrey
15 J4 **Elstree** Herts
37 G3 **Elterwater** Cumb
16 B2 **Eltisley** Cambs
23 L2 **Elton** Cambs
24 F7 **Elveden** Suffk
14 E7 **Elvetham Heath**
Hants
34 D3 **Elvington** York
5 J4 **Elworthy** Somset
24 C7 **Ely** Cambs
47 M7 **Embleton** Nthumb
64 E8 **Embo** Highld
30 F8 **Empingham** Rutlnd
9 H5 **Emsworth** Hants
22 F1 **Enderby** Leics
15 K4 **Enfield** Gt Lon
36 D2 **Ennerdale Bridge**
Cumb
14 B2 **Enstone** Oxon
16 C6 **Epping** Essex
15 J7 **Epsom** Surrey
34 E6 **Epworth** N Linc
58 E6 **Errogie** Highld
51 H4 **Errol** P & K
20 E6 **Erwood** Powys
15 H7 **Esher** Surrey
36 E4 **Eskdale Green** Cumb
42 A3 **Eskdalemuir** D & G
31 G8 **Essendine** Rutlnd
15 J3 **Essendon** Herts
38 E2 **Eston** R & Cl
47 J6 **Etal** Nthumb

10 F5	**Etchingham** E Susx	
15 G6	**Eton** W & M	
22 D5	**Ettington** Warwks	
46 D7	**Ettrick** Border	
46 E7	**Ettrickbridge** Border	
58 E3	**Evanton** Highld	
13 G7	**Evercreech** Somset	
14 E7	**Eversley** Hants	
22 B6	**Evesham** Worcs	
13 K2	**Ewen** Gloucs	
9 K2	**Ewhurst** Surrey	
21 H7	**Ewyas Harold** Herefs	
5 H5	**Exebridge** Somset	
6 C3	**Exeter** Devon	
5 H4	**Exford** Somset	
6 C3	**Exminster** Devon	
6 D4	**Exmouth** Devon	
23 M1	**Eye** C Pete	
25 H7	**Eye** Suffk	
47 J4	**Eyemouth** Border	
10 D2	**Eynsford** Kent	
14 B3	**Eynsham** Oxon	

F

33 H6	**Failsworth** Oldham	
26 E8	**Fairbourne** Gwynd	
13 L2	**Fairford** Gloucs	
44 F3	**Fairlie** N Ayrs	
11 G6	**Fairlight** E Susx	
24 F3	**Fakenham** Norfk	
46 E4	**Fala** Mdloth	
31 G2	**Faldingworth** Lincs	
13 G3	**Falfield** S Glos	
50 E8	**Falkirk** Falk	
51 H6	**Falkland** Fife	
2 E7	**Falmouth** Cnwll	
42 E3	**Falstone** Nthumb	
37 G4	**Far Sawrey** Cumb	
8 F5	**Fareham** Hants	
14 A4	**Faringdon** Oxon	
14 F7	**Farnborough** Hants	
51 L2	**Farnell** Angus	
9 H2	**Farnham** Surrey	
15 G5	**Farnham Common** Bucks	
10 D2	**Farningham** Kent	
45 M2	**Fauldhouse** W Loth	
11 H3	**Faversham** Kent	
8 E5	**Fawley** Hants	
22 C1	**Fazeley** Staffs	
50 C3	**Fearnan** P & K	
17 K4	**Felixstowe** Suffk	
16 E5	**Felsted** Essex	
43 J2	**Felton** Nthumb	
24 E6	**Feltwell** Norfk	
29 J5	**Fenny Bentley** Derbys	
6 E3	**Fenny Bridges** Devon	
22 E6	**Fenny Compton** Warwks	
22 E1	**Fenny Drayton** Leics	
45 H4	**Fenwick** E Ayrs	
8 B5	**Ferndown** Dorset	
21 M4	**Fernhill Heath** Worcs	
9 J3	**Fernhurst** W Susx	
29 G3	**Fernilee** Derbys	
9 K5	**Ferring** W Susx	
43 K8	**Ferryhill** Dur	
55 K6	**Fettercairn** Abers	
26 F5	**Ffestiniog** Gwynd	
25 L4	**Filby** Norfk	
39 K5	**Filey** N York	
24 E5	**Fincham** Norfk	
16 E4	**Finchingfield** Essex	
59 J3	**Findhorn** Moray	
60 C3	**Findochty** Moray	
9 L5	**Findon** W Susx	
23 J3	**Finedon** Nhants	
17 H1	**Finningham** Suffk	

34 D6	**Finningley** Donc	
65 b4	**Finstown** Ork	
50 B7	**Fintry** Stirlg	
48 C2	**Fionnphort** Ag & B	
8 F6	**Fishbourne** IOW	
18 C3	**Fishguard** Pembks	
9 K4	**Fittleworth** W Susx	
5 K4	**Fitzhead** Somset	
7 c2	**Five Oaks** Jersey	
61 c6	**Fladdabister** Shet	
39 L6	**Flamborough** E R Yk	
15 H3	**Flamstead** Herts	
14 F7	**Fleet** Hants	
32 C3	**Fleetwood** Lancs	
41 K7	**Flimby** Cumb	
27 K3	**Flint** Flints	
23 K6	**Flitwick** Beds	
39 K5	**Flixton** N York	
23 G4	**Flore** Nhants	
59 K6	**Fochabers** Moray	
11 K5	**Folkestone** Kent	
31 G6	**Folkingham** Lincs	
7 L1	**Fontmell Magna** Dorset	
9 J5	**Fontwell** W Susx	
49 G3	**Ford** Ag & B	
47 J6	**Ford** Nthumb	
10 D4	**Fordcombe** Kent	
8 C4	**Fordingbridge** Hants	
55 K6	**Fordoun** Abers	
11 J3	**Fordwich** Kent	
6 a2	**Forest** Guern	
10 C5	**Forest Row** E Susx	
51 J2	**Forfar** Angus	
32 C6	**Formby** Sefton	
59 J4	**Forres** Moray	
58 C7	**Fort Augustus** Highld	
54 D8	**Fort William** Highld	
50 F5	**Forteviot** P & K	
45 M3	**Forth** S Lans	
50 C3	**Fortingall** P & K	
32 E2	**Forton** Lancs	
58 F4	**Fortrose** Highld	
7 J4	**Fortuneswell** Dorset	
30 E5	**Foston** Lincs	
27 L7	**Four Crosses** Powys	
9 G3	**Four Marks** Hants	
3 G5	**Fowey** Cnwll	
21 J6	**Fownhope** Herefs	
36 b3	**Foxdale** IOM	
58 D7	**Foyers** Highld	
17 K2	**Framlingham** Suffk	
7 J3	**Frampton** Dorset	
10 E5	**Frant** E Susx	
61 G3	**Fraserburgh** Abers	
24 D8	**Freckenham** Suffk	
32 D4	**Freckleton** Lancs	
9 H2	**Frensham** Surrey	
8 D6	**Freshwater** IOW	
25 J7	**Fressingfield** Suffk	
65 J2	**Freswick** Highld	
39 H7	**Fridaythorpe** E R Yk	
14 B4	**Frilford** Oxon	
17 K5	**Frinton-on-Sea** Essex	
51 K2	**Friockheim** Angus	
25 L5	**Fritton** Norfk	
36 D2	**Frizington** Cumb	
13 H2	**Frocester** Gloucs	
28 C3	**Frodsham** Ches	
7 K2	**Frome** Somset	
14 A6	**Froxfield** Wilts	
9 H5	**Funtington** W Susx	
49 J4	**Furnace** Ag & B	
29 G2	**Furness Vale** Derbys	
16 D6	**Fyfield** Essex	
14 B4	**Fyfield** Oxon	
60 E5	**Fyvie** Abers	

G

28 F8	**Gailey** Staffs	

38 B2	**Gainford** Dur	
34 E7	**Gainsborough** Lincs	
57 H2	**Gairloch** Highld	
53 J3	**Gairlochy** Highld	
46 E6	**Galashiels** Border	
37 H7	**Galgate** Lancs	
45 H4	**Galston** E Ayrs	
16 B3	**Gamlingay** Cambs	
30 D3	**Gamston** Notts	
26 F7	**Ganllwyd** Gwynd	
25 G7	**Garboldisham** Norfk	
60 E3	**Gardenstown** Abers	
49 K4	**Garelochhead** Ag & B	
34 B4	**Garforth** Leeds	
33 H2	**Gargrave** N York	
40 F6	**Garlieston** D & G	
55 L4	**Garlogie** Abers	
42 E7	**Garrigill** Cumb	
32 E3	**Garstang** Lancs	
20 D5	**Garth** Powys	
46 F3	**Garvald** E Loth	
58 C3	**Garve** Highld	
41 G6	**Gatehouse of Fleet** D & G	
43 K5	**Gateshead** Gatesd	
22 E5	**Gaydon** Warwks	
24 E4	**Gayton** Norfk	
31 K6	**Gedney Drove End** Lincs	
31 J8	**Gedney Hill** Lincs	
4 D4	**Georgeham** Devon	
15 G5	**Gerrards Cross** Bucks	
46 F3	**Gifford** E Loth	
37 L6	**Giggleswick** N York	
38 B3	**Gilling West** N York	
13 H8	**Gillingham** Dorset	
10 F2	**Gillingham** Medway	
25 L6	**Gillingham** Norfk	
65 J1	**Gills** Highld	
50 E4	**Gilmerton** P & K	
42 E5	**Gilsland** Nthumb	
21 G8	**Gilwern** Mons	
16 C2	**Girton** Cambs	
40 C3	**Girvan** S Ayrs	
33 G2	**Gisburn** Lancs	
51 J3	**Glamis** Angus	
42 K7	**Glanton** Nthumb	
30 B3	**Glapwell** Derbys	
20 F6	**Glasbury** Powys	
45 J2	**Glasgow** C Glas	
23 J1	**Glaston** Rutlnd	
12 F7	**Glastonbury** Somset	
17 G3	**Glemsford** Suffk	
36 b3	**Glen Maye** IOM	
44 B4	**Glenbarr** Ag & B	
52 D5	**Glenborrodale** Highld	
41 K5	**Glencaple** D & G	
53 H5	**Glencoe** Highld	
49 H5	**Glendaruel** Ag & B	
50 E6	**Glendevon** P & K	
50 E6	**Gleneagles** P & K	
57 H7	**Glenelg** Highld	
51 G5	**Glenfarg** P & K	
52 F3	**Glenfinnan** Highld	
55 H3	**Glenkindie** Abers	
40 C6	**Glenluce** D & G	
37 G2	**Glenridding** Cumb	
51 H6	**Glenrothes** Fife	
35 G7	**Glentham** Lincs	
33 J7	**Glossop** Derbys	
21 M7	**Gloucester** Gloucs	
27 K6	**Glyn Ceiriog** Wrexhm	
19 L5	**Glyn-Neath** Neath	
19 L6	**Glyncorrwg** Neath	
10 C7	**Glynde** E Susx	
20 C8	**Glyntawe** Powys	
28 F7	**Gnosall** Staffs	
39 H3	**Goathland** N York	
12 D7	**Goathurst** Somset	
27 L6	**Gobowen** Shrops	
9 J2	**Godalming** Surrey	

23 M4	**Godmanchester** Cambs	
8 F7	**Godshill** IOW	
10 C3	**Godstone** Surrey	
20 B3	**Goginan** Cerdgn	
32 F6	**Golborne** Wigan	
17 G6	**Goldhanger** Essex	
64 E7	**Golspie** Highld	
9 K2	**Gomshall** Surrey	
34 E4	**Goole** E R Yk	
28 E3	**Goostrey** Ches	
47 G5	**Gordon** Border	
46 D4	**Gorebridge** Mdloth	
7 c1	**Gorey** Jersey	
14 D5	**Goring** Oxon	
2 F6	**Gorran Haven** Cnwll	
19 J6	**Gorseinon** Swans	
31 H6	**Gosberton** Lincs	
36 D3	**Gosforth** Cumb	
43 J5	**Gosforth** N u Ty	
8 F5	**Gosport** Hants	
10 F4	**Goudhurst** Kent	
49 K5	**Gourock** Inver	
19 J6	**Gowerton** Swans	
35 H3	**Goxhill** E R Yk	
35 H5	**Goxhill** N Linc	
11 G2	**Grain** Medway	
35 K6	**Grainthorpe** Lincs	
2 F6	**Grampound** Cnwll	
6 a1	**Grandes Rocques** Guern	
36 F2	**Grange** Cumb	
37 G5	**Grange-over-Sands** Cumb	
50 E8	**Grangemouth** Falk	
30 F6	**Grantham** Lincs	
59 J6	**Grantown-on-Spey** Highld	
47 H4	**Grantshouse** Border	
37 G3	**Grasmere** Cumb	
38 A6	**Grassington** N York	
16 B4	**Graveley** Herts	
10 E2	**Gravesend** Kent	
10 E1	**Grays** Thurr	
37 J3	**Great Asby** Cumb	
38 F3	**Great Ayton** N York	
13 H3	**Great Badminton** S Glos	
16 E4	**Great Bardfield** Essex	
23 L5	**Great Barford** Beds	
24 E3	**Great Bircham** Norfk	
17 J3	**Great Blakenham** Suffk	
30 F8	**Great Casterton** Rutlnd	
16 D3	**Great Chesterford** Essex	
30 D7	**Great Dalby** Leics	
16 E5	**Great Dunmow** Essex	
8 B3	**Great Durnford** Wilts	
23 L3	**Great Gidding** Cambs	
16 B2	**Great Gransden** Cambs	
33 G4	**Great Harwood** Lancs	
29 G7	**Great Haywood** Staffs	
25 G6	**Great Hockham** Norfk	
14 F3	**Great Kimble** Bucks	
36 F3	**Great Langdale** Cumb	
21 L5	**Great Malvern** Worcs	
24 E4	**Great Massingham** Norfk	
14 F4	**Great Missenden** Bucks	
30 F6	**Great Ponton** Lincs	
16 E4	**Great Sampford** Essex	
28 B3	**Great Saughall** Ches	
14 B6	**Great Shefford** W Berk	

16 C3 Great Shelford Cambs
38 D3 Great Smeaton N York
22 E7 Great Tew Oxon
4 E5 Great Torrington Devon
17 G8 Great Wakering Essex
16 E6 Great Waltham Essex
21 L4 Great Witley Worcs
25 L5 Great Yarmouth Norfk
16 F4 Great Yeldham Essex
9 H3 Greatham Hants
38 E7 Green Hammerton N York
27 K3 Greenfield Flints
42 E5 Greenhead Nthumb
38 B6 Greenhow Hill N York
47 G5 Greenlaw Border
50 D6 Greenloaning P & K
49 L5 Greenock Inver
36 F5 Greenodd Cumb
30 F7 Greetham Rutlnd
27 L4 Gresford Wrexhm
38 B3 Greta Bridge Dur
42 B5 Gretna D & G
42 B5 Gretna Green D & G
42 C8 Greystoke Cumb
35 J5 Grimsby NE Lin
31 G7 Grimsthorpe Lincs
29 J3 Grindleford Derbys
34 E7 Gringley on the Hill Notts
30 B8 Groby Leics
21 H7 Grosmont Mons
39 H3 Grosmont N York
7 c2 Grouville Jersey
14 B5 Grove Oxon
51 J5 Guardbridge Fife
11 G6 Guestling Green E Susx
9 K2 Guildford Surrey
38 F2 Guisborough R & Cl
33 K3 Guiseley Leeds
25 G4 Guist Norfk
46 E2 Gullane E Loth
34 E5 Gunness N Linc
3 K4 Gunnislake Cnwll
30 D5 Gunthorpe Notts
8 E6 Gurnard IOW
8 A5 Gussage All Saints Dorset
61 d2 Gutcher Shet
24 B5 Guyhirn Cambs
2 D7 Gweek Cnwll
27 K4 Gwernymynydd Flints
2 C6 Gwithian Cnwll
27 J5 Gwyddelwern Denbgs

H

65 b3 Hackland Ork
39 J4 Hackness N York
15 K5 Hackney Gt Lon
14 E3 Haddenham Bucks
24 C7 Haddenham Cambs
46 F3 Haddington E Loth
25 L6 Haddiscoe Norfk
17 H3 Hadleigh Suffk
10 E4 Hadlow Kent
31 J3 Hagworthingham Lincs
10 E7 Hailsham E Susx
5 J6 Halberton Devon
25 K6 Hales Norfk
22 A3 Halesowen Dudley

25 K7 Halesworth Suffk
33 K4 Halifax Calder
65 G2 Halkirk Highld
6 B7 Hallsands Devon
16 F4 Halstead Essex
10 D3 Halstead Kent
42 E5 Haltwhistle Nthumb
6 B6 Halwell Devon
4 D7 Halwill Junction Devon
8 E5 Hamble-le-Rice Hants
9 G4 Hambledon Hants
32 D3 Hambleton Lancs
45 K3 Hamilton S Lans
15 J6 Hammersmith Gt Lon
14 C6 Hampstead Norrey's W Berk
38 C7 Hampsthwaite N York
14 B7 Hamstead Marshall W Berk
11 H5 Hamstreet Kent
10 B5 Handcross W Susx
28 C4 Handley Ches
28 F5 Hanley C Stke
25 K3 Happisburgh Norfk
6 B6 Harbertonford Devon
13 H1 Hardwicke Gloucs
16 C4 Hare Street Herts
33 L3 Harewood Leeds
21 J7 Harewood End Herefs
26 E6 Harlech Gwynd
25 J7 Harleston Norfk
56 C5 Harlosh Highld
16 C6 Harlow Essex
2 E4 Harlyn Cnwll
61 d1 Haroldswick Shet
38 F5 Harome N York
15 H3 Harpenden Herts
33 L2 Harrogate N York
23 K5 Harrold Beds
15 H5 Harrow Gt Lon
16 C3 Harston Cambs
43 H3 Hartburn Nthumb
17 G3 Hartest Suffk
10 D5 Hartfield E Susx
29 H4 Hartington Derbys
4 C5 Hartland Devon
43 M8 Hartlepool Hartpl
14 E7 Hartley Wintney Hants
21 L7 Hartpury Gloucs
22 B5 Harvington Worcs
17 K4 Harwich Essex
22 D4 Haseley Warwks
9 J3 Haslemere Surrey
10 F7 Hastings E Susx
12 D8 Hatch Beauchamp Somset
34 D5 Hatfield Donc
15 J3 Hatfield Herts
16 D5 Hatfield Broad Oak Essex
16 D5 Hatfield Heath Essex
16 F6 Hatfield Peverel Essex
4 E6 Hatherleigh Devon
30 B7 Hathern Leics
29 J2 Hathersage Derbys
61 H5 Hatton Abers
9 G5 Havant Hants
8 F6 Havenstreet IOW
18 C5 Haverfordwest Pembks
16 E3 Haverhill Suffk
27 L3 Hawarden Flints
31 H4 Hawes N York
46 F7 Hawick Border
16 F3 Hawkedon Suffk

10 F5 Hawkhurst Kent
11 K4 Hawkinge Kent
37 G4 Hawkshead Cumb
38 E4 Hawnby N York
33 J3 Haworth Brad
38 F7 Haxby N York
34 E6 Haxey N Linc
21 G6 Hay-on-Wye Powys
42 F5 Haydon Bridge Nthumb
2 C6 Hayle Cnwll
10 B6 Haywards Heath W Susx
28 F2 Hazel Grove Stockp
24 D3 Heacham Norfk
11 G4 Headcorn Kent
29 L5 Heanor Derbys
29 L3 Heath Derbys
29 G8 Heath Hayes & Wimblebury Staffs
10 E6 Heathfield E Susx
29 G4 Heaton Staffs
31 G5 Heckington Lincs
8 E4 Hedge End Hants
29 G8 Hednesford Staffs
35 H4 Hedon E R Yk
49 L5 Helensburgh Ag & B
37 L7 Hellifield N York
17 K2 Helmingham Suffk
65 G6 Helmsdale Highld
38 F5 Helmsley N York
31 G5 Helpringham Lincs
28 C3 Helsby Ches
2 C7 Helston Cnwll
15 H3 Hemel Hempstead Herts
24 A8 Hemingford Abbots Cambs
25 J6 Hempnall Norfk
25 L4 Hemsby Norfk
34 B5 Hemsworth Wakefd
5 K6 Hemyock Devon
19 J6 Hendy Carmth
9 L4 Henfield W Susx
16 D4 Henham Essex
22 C4 Henley-in-Arden Warwks
14 E5 Henley-on-Thames Oxon
27 J3 Henllan Denbgs
23 L6 Henlow Beds
25 L7 Henstead Suffk
7 K1 Henstridge Somset
21 J6 Hereford Herefs
14 C6 Hermitage W Berk
11 J2 Herne Bay Kent
11 K3 Hersden Kent
10 E6 Herstmonceux E Susx
15 K3 Hertford Herts
35 G4 Hessle E R Yk
27 L2 Heswall Wirral
25 H5 Hethersett Norfk
37 H5 Heversham Cumb
43 G5 Hexham Nthumb
3 M4 Hexworthy Devon
3 K6 Heybrook Bay Devon
37 G7 Heysham Lancs
13 J6 Heytesbury Wilts
35 G6 Hibaldstow N Linc
10 B6 Hickstead W Susx
37 J6 High Bentham N York
28 D7 High Ercall Wrekin
11 G5 High Halden Kent
42 C7 High Hesket Cumb
16 E5 High Roding Essex
14 F4 High Wycombe Bucks
23 K4 Higham Ferrers Nhants
4 E6 Highampton Devon
12 D6 Highbridge Somset
14 B7 Highclere Hants
2 b1 Higher Town IOS

21 L3 Highley Shrops
13 M3 Highworth Swindn
10 D4 Hildenborough Kent
9 H3 Hill Brow Hants
59 G2 Hill of Fearn Highld
61 b3 Hillswick Shet
13 K4 Hilmarton Wilts
37 K2 Hilton Cumb
22 E2 Hinckley Leics
39 G2 Hinderwell N York
9 J3 Hindhead Surrey
13 J7 Hindon Wilts
25 G5 Hingham Norfk
38 B4 Hipswell N York
12 A2 Hirwaun Rhondd
16 C2 Histon Cambs
17 H3 Hitcham Suffk
23 M7 Hitchin Herts
17 G7 Hockley Essex
23 K7 Hockliffe Beds
15 K3 Hoddesdon Herts
28 D6 Hodnet Shrops
31 L3 Hogsthorpe Lincs
31 J7 Holbeach Lincs
3 L5 Holbeton Devon
17 J4 Holbrook Suffk
8 E5 Holbury Hants
24 F2 Holkham Norfk
11 G3 Hollingbourne Kent
9 L2 Holmbury St Mary Surrey
34 E3 Holme upon Spalding Moor E R Yk
28 E3 Holmes Chapel Ches
33 K6 Holmfirth Kirk
36 D4 Holmrook Cumb
6 A5 Holne Devon
4 C6 Holsworthy Devon
25 H3 Holt Norfk
13 J5 Holt Wilts
28 B4 Holt Wrexhm
21 L4 Holt Heath Worcs
35 J6 Holton le Clay Lincs
47 L5 Holy Island Nthumb
8 B5 Holyhead IOA
45 L2 Holytown N Lans
7 J2 Holywell Dorset
27 K3 Holywell Flints
25 J7 Homersfield Suffk
25 H5 Honingham Norfk
24 F7 Honington Suffk
6 E2 Honiton Devon
10 F2 Hoo St Werburgh Medway
14 E7 Hook Hants
29 J2 Hope Derbys
6 A7 Hope Devon
27 L4 Hope Flints
21 J2 Hope Bowdler Shrops
21 J5 Hope under Dinmore Herefs
59 K3 Hopeman Moray
25 L5 Hopton on Sea Norfk
10 D6 Horam E Susx
10 D6 Horley Surrey
37 J6 Hornby Lancs
31 H3 Horncastle Lincs
9 G4 Horndean Hants
4 D5 Horns Cross Devon
35 H3 Hornsea E R Yk
3 L4 Horrabridge Devon
25 L4 Horsey Norfk
9 L3 Horsham W Susx
43 H5 Horsley Nthumb
8 B5 Horton Dorset
6 F1 Horton Somset
37 K6 Horton in Ribblesdale N York
14 D3 Horton-cum-Studley Oxon
32 F5 Horwich Bolton
30 C7 Hoton Leics

43 K6	**Houghton le Spring** Sundld
23 G1	**Houghton on the Hill** Leics
25 G3	**Houghton St Giles** Norfk
15 H6	**Hounslow** Gt Lon
65 b4	**Houton** Ork
10 B7	**Hove** Br & H
38 F5	**Hovingham** N York
34 E4	**Howden** E R Yk
25 J7	**Hoxne** Suffk
32 B7	**Hoylake** Wirral
34 B6	**Hoyland Nether** Barns
30 B5	**Hucknall** Notts
33 K5	**Huddersfield** Kirk
2 a2	**Hugh Town** IOS
35 J6	**Humberston** NE Lin
46 E4	**Humbie** E Loth
47 G5	**Hume** Border
14 B6	**Hungerford** W Berk
39 K5	**Hunmanby** N York
24 D2	**Hunstanton** Norfk
23 M3	**Huntingdon** Cambs
21 L7	**Huntley** Gloucs
60 C5	**Huntly** Abers
8 E4	**Hursley** Hants
10 F5	**Hurst Green** E Susx
32 F3	**Hurst Green** Lancs
8 E2	**Hurstbourne Priors** Hants
14 B7	**Hurstbourne Tarrant** Hants
10 B6	**Hurstpierpoint** W Susx
38 C3	**Hurworth-on-Tees** Darltn
23 G2	**Husbands Bosworth** Leics
23 K6	**Husborne Crawley** Beds
31 L3	**Huttoft** Lincs
39 G4	**Hutton-le-Hole** N York
33 H7	**Hyde** Tamesd
48 b3	**Hynish** Ag & B
8 E5	**Hythe** Hants
11 J5	**Hythe** Kent

I

29 K8	**Ibstock** Leics
6 C4	**Ideford** Devon
12 F8	**Ilchester** Somset
4 E3	**Ilfracombe** Devon
29 L5	**Ilkeston** Derbys
33 K3	**Ilkley** Brad
7 G1	**Ilminster** Somset
35 H5	**Immingham** NE Lin
35 H5	**Immingham Dock** NE Lin
63 H5	**Inchnadamph** Highld
16 E2	**Ingatestone** Essex
30 F2	**Ingham** Lincs
37 K6	**Ingleton** N York
24 E3	**Ingoldisthorpe** Norfk
31 L3	**Ingoldmells** Lincs
22 B5	**Inkberrow** Worcs
49 K6	**Innellan** Ag & B
46 D6	**Innerleithen** Border
60 D6	**Insch** Abers
54 C4	**Insh** Highld
4 D4	**Instow** Devon
61 G3	**Inverallochy** Abers
64 C7	**Inveran** Highld
49 J3	**Inveraray** Ag & B
57 H2	**Inverasdale** Highld
55 L6	**Inverbervie** Abers
53 K2	**Invergarry** Highld

58 F3	**Invergordon** Highld
51 H4	**Invergowrie** P & K
57 J6	**Inverinate** Highld
51 L2	**Inverkeilor** Angus
46 B2	**Inverkeithing** Fife
60 D5	**Inverkeithny** Abers
49 K6	**Inverkip** Inver
58 D7	**Invermoriston** Highld
58 F5	**Inverness** Highld
55 L3	**Inverurie** Abers
6 B5	**Ipplepen** Devon
29 G5	**Ipstones** Staffs
17 J3	**Ipswich** Suffk
23 J4	**Irchester** Nhants
42 A7	**Ireby** Cumb
21 K1	**Ironbridge** Wrekin
23 K3	**Irthlingborough** Nhants
45 G4	**Irvine** N Ayrs
40 F7	**Isle of Whithorn** D & G
57 G2	**Isleornsay** Highld
15 K5	**Islington** Gt Lon
8 F3	**Itchen Abbas** Hants
15 G5	**Iver** Bucks
15 G3	**Ivinghoe** Bucks
5 M5	**Ivybridge** Devon
11 G2	**Iwade** Kent
7 L1	**Iwerne Minster** Dorset
25 G8	**Ixworth** Suffk

J

43 K5	**Jarrow** S Tyne
47 G7	**Jedburgh** Border
6 b2	**Jerbourg** Guern
10 D7	**Jevington** E Susx
65 J1	**John o'Groats** Highld
55 L7	**Johnshaven** Abers
18 C5	**Johnston** Pembks
49 M6	**Johnstone** Rens
36 c1	**Jurby** IOM

K

49 H6	**Kames** Ag & B
35 H5	**Keelby** Lincs
30 B6	**Kegworth** Leics
33 J3	**Keighley** Brad
65 J2	**Keiss** Highld
60 B4	**Keith** Moray
37 L3	**Keld** N York
30 D4	**Kelham** Notts
47 G6	**Kelso** Border
17 G5	**Kelvedon** Essex
13 K2	**Kemble** Gloucs
55 K3	**Kemnay** Abers
23 K5	**Kempston** Beds
37 H4	**Kendal** Cumb
22 B4	**Kenilworth** Warwks
50 D3	**Kenmore** P & K
49 G6	**Kennacraig** Ag & B
6 C3	**Kennford** Devon
25 G7	**Kenninghall** Norfk
53 G5	**Kentallen** Highld
16 F2	**Kentford** Suffk
6 C4	**Kenton** Devon
20 F2	**Kerry** Powys
25 L6	**Kessingland** Suffk
36 F2	**Keswick** Cumb
23 J3	**Kettering** Nhants
37 M6	**Kettlewell** N York
23 K1	**Ketton** Rutlnd
10 B6	**Keymer** W Susx
13 G4	**Keynsham** BaNES
23 K3	**Keyston** Cambs
30 C6	**Keyworth** Notts

23 G2	**Kibworth Harcourt** Leics
21 M3	**Kidderminster** Worcs
14 C3	**Kidlington** Oxon
28 F4	**Kidsgrove** Staffs
19 G5	**Kidwelly** Carmth
42 D3	**Kielder** Nthumb
48 F6	**Kilberry** Ag & B
45 G3	**Kilbirnie** N Ayrs
29 K5	**Kilburn** Derbys
38 E5	**Kilburn** N York
44 E3	**Kilchattan** Ag & B
52 C4	**Kilchoan** Highld
49 J2	**Kilchrenan** Ag & B
49 K5	**Kilcreggan** Ag & B
38 F3	**Kildale** N York
55 H3	**Kildrummy** Abers
33 J3	**Kildwick** N York
49 H5	**Kilfinan** Ag & B
18 E5	**Kilgetty** Pembks
39 K6	**Kilham** E R Yk
44 B5	**Kilkenzie** Ag & B
4 C6	**Kilkhampton** Cnwll
50 B7	**Killearn** Stirlg
54 D7	**Killiecrankie** P & K
50 B4	**Killin** Stirlg
49 L6	**Kilmacolm** Inver
51 J5	**Kilmany** Fife
45 H4	**Kilmarnock** E Ayrs
49 G4	**Kilmartin** Ag & B
45 H4	**Kilmaurs** E Ayrs
49 G3	**Kilmelford** Ag & B
58 D5	**Kilmorack** Highld
49 G2	**Kilninver** Ag & B
51 K6	**Kilrenny** Fife
50 C8	**Kilsyth** N Lans
5 K3	**Kilve** Somset
45 G4	**Kilwinning** N Ayrs
25 H5	**Kimberley** Norfk
23 L4	**Kimbolton** Cambs
64 E5	**Kinbrace** Highld
50 E7	**Kincardine** Fife
55 J4	**Kincardine O'Neil** Abers
54 C4	**Kincraig** Highld
22 E5	**Kineton** Warwks
23 K1	**King's Cliffe** Nhants
24 D4	**King's Lynn** Norfk
6 a2	**King's Mills** Guern
8 D3	**King's Somborne** Hants
7 K2	**King's Stag** Dorset
13 H2	**King's Stanley** Gloucs
15 H4	**Kings Langley** Herts
8 E3	**Kings Worthy** Hants
51 K5	**Kingsbarns** Fife
6 B7	**Kingsbridge** Devon
22 D2	**Kingsbury** Warwks
14 C7	**Kingsclere** Hants
11 L4	**Kingsdown** Kent
9 L3	**Kingsfold** W Susx
6 C5	**Kingskerswell** Devon
21 H4	**Kingsland** Herefs
29 G5	**Kingsley** Staffs
11 H4	**Kingsnorth** Kent
6 C4	**Kingsteignton** Devon
59 L3	**Kingston on Spey** Moray
35 G4	**Kingston upon Hull** C KuH
15 J6	**Kingston upon Thames** Gt Lon
21 H6	**Kingstone** Herefs
6 C6	**Kingswear** Devon
21 G5	**Kington** Herefs
54 B4	**Kingussie** Highld
57 J8	**Kinloch Hourn** Highld
50 C2	**Kinloch Rannoch** P & K
63 H3	**Kinlochbervie** Highld
53 G1	**Kinlocheil** Highld
57 J3	**Kinlochewe** Highld

53 J5	**Kinlochleven** Highld
59 J3	**Kinloss** Moray
55 L6	**Kinneff** Abers
50 F6	**Kinross** P & K
14 B6	**Kintbury** W Berk
55 L3	**Kintore** Abers
50 C7	**Kippen** Stirlg
39 G5	**Kirby Misperton** N York
22 F1	**Kirby Muxloe** Leics
29 K6	**Kirk Langley** Derbys
36 b2	**Kirk Michael** IOM
61 c6	**Kirkabister** Shet
41 K6	**Kirkbean** D & G
42 A6	**Kirkbride** Cumb
33 K5	**Kirkburton** Kirk
52 D6	**Kirkby** Knows
30 B4	**Kirkby in Ashfield** Notts
37 J5	**Kirkby Lonsdale** Cumb
38 C5	**Kirkby Malzeard** N York
37 K3	**Kirkby Stephen** Cumb
37 J2	**Kirkby Thore** Cumb
39 G5	**Kirkbymoorside** N York
51 H7	**Kirkcaldy** Fife
40 B5	**Kirkcolm** D & G
45 K6	**Kirkconnel** D & G
40 D5	**Kirkcowan** D & G
41 G6	**Kirkcudbright** D & G
32 D4	**Kirkham** Lancs
58 E5	**Kirkhill** Highld
40 E6	**Kirkinner** D & G
45 K1	**Kirkintilloch** E Duns
50 F2	**Kirkmichael** P & K
45 G6	**Kirkmichael** S Ayrs
47 J6	**Kirknewton** Nthumb
42 D7	**Kirkoswald** Cumb
44 F6	**Kirkoswald** S Ayrs
36 b3	**Kirkpatrick** IOM
41 H5	**Kirkpatrick Durham** D & G
42 B5	**Kirkpatrick-Fleming** D & G
55 L4	**Kirkton of Skene** Abers
65 c4	**Kirkwall** Ork
43 H4	**Kirkwhelpington** Nthumb
51 J2	**Kirriemuir** Angus
31 J6	**Kirton** Lincs
34 F6	**Kirton in Lindsey** N Linc
23 H4	**Kislingbury** Nhants
38 D7	**Knaresborough** N York
42 E6	**Knarsdale** Nthumb
15 J2	**Knebworth** Herts
21 G3	**Knighton** Powys
21 L5	**Knightwick** Worcs
63 H6	**Knockan** Highld
27 L7	**Knockin** Shrops
34 C4	**Knottingley** Wakefd
14 F5	**Knowl Hill** W & M
28 E3	**Knutsford** Ches
57 G6	**Kyle of Lochalsh** Highld
57 G6	**Kyleakin** Highld
57 G7	**Kylerhea** Highld

L

6 b1	**L'Ancresse** Guern
6 a2	**L'Eree** Guern
7 a1	**L'Etacq** Jersey
7 a1	**La Greve de Lecq** Jersey

35 H6 **Laceby** NE Lin
2 E5 **Ladock** Cnwll
51 H5 **Ladybank** Fife
54 A5 **Laggan** Highld
62 E8 **Laide** Highld
64 C6 **Lairg** Highld
24 E7 **Lakenheath** Suffk
10 E5 **Lamberhurst** Kent
14 B6 **Lambourn** W Berk
3 K3 **Lamerton** Devon
46 A6 **Lamington** S Lans
44 D5 **Lamlash** N Ayrs
19 J2 **Lampeter** Cerdgn
23 H3 **Lamport** Nhants
45 M4 **Lanark** S Lans
37 H6 **Lancaster** Lancs
43 J6 **Lanchester** Dur
9 L5 **Lancing** W Susx
3 J5 **Landrake** Cnwll
30 E8 **Langham** Rutlnd
42 B4 **Langholm** D & G
12 E8 **Langport** Somset
38 A3 **Langthwaite** N York
39 J6 **Langtoft** E R Yk
8 A7 **Langton Matravers** Dorset
42 D7 **Langwathby** Cumb
31 G3 **Langworth** Lincs
3 G4 **Lanivet** Cnwll
5 G6 **Lapford** Devon
51 J6 **Largoward** Fife
44 F2 **Largs** N Ayrs
45 L3 **Larkhall** S Lans
8 B2 **Larkhill** Wilts
39 G4 **Lastingham** N York
17 G7 **Latchingdon** Essex
65 H4 **Latheron** Highld
46 F5 **Lauder** Border
18 F5 **Laugharne** Carmth
3 J3 **Launceston** Cnwll
55 K6 **Laurencekirk** Abers
41 G5 **Laurieston** D & G
17 G3 **Lavenham** Suffk
50 C3 **Lawers** P & K
36 c3 **Laxey** IOM
25 K8 **Laxfield** Suffk
42 D7 **Lazonby** Cumb
16 E6 **Leaden Roding** Essex
30 F5 **Leadenham** Lincs
43 J6 **Leadgate** Dur
45 M6 **Leadhills** S Lans
22 D4 **Leamington Spa** Warwks
15 H7 **Leatherhead** Surrey
13 M2 **Lechlade** Gloucs
21 L6 **Ledbury** Herefs
4 E3 **Lee** Devon
8 F5 **Lee-on-the-Solent** Hants
21 J1 **Leebotwood** Shrops
33 L4 **Leeds** Leeds
29 G4 **Leek** Staffs
38 C4 **Leeming Bar** N York
31 J2 **Legbourne** Lincs
23 G1 **Leicester** C Leic
10 D4 **Leigh** Kent
32 F6 **Leigh** Wigan
21 L5 **Leigh Sinton** Worcs
23 J7 **Leighton Buzzard** Beds
21 H3 **Leintwardine** Herefs
17 M2 **Leiston** Suffk
2 C6 **Lelant** Cnwll
40 C3 **Lendalfoot** S Ayrs
11 G3 **Lenham** Kent
50 B8 **Lennoxtown** E Duns
21 J4 **Leominster** Herefs
61 c6 **Lerwick** Shet
60 D6 **Leslie** Abers
51 H6 **Leslie** Fife
45 L4 **Lesmahagow** S Lans
40 B5 **Leswalt** D & G

16 B4 **Letchworth** Herts
51 K3 **Letham** Angus
18 C4 **Letterston** Pembks
51 J5 **Leuchars** Fife
35 H3 **Leven** E R Yk
51 J6 **Leven** Fife
37 H5 **Levens** Cumb
62 e7 **Leverburgh** W Isls
10 C7 **Lewes** E Susx
38 B4 **Leyburn** N York
32 E5 **Leyland** Lancs
11 H2 **Leysdown-on-Sea** Kent
59 L3 **Lhanbryde** Moray
46 A5 **Libberton** S Lans
29 H8 **Lichfield** Staffs
16 F2 **Lidgate** Suffk
3 J3 **Lifton** Devon
15 G7 **Lightwater** Surrey
46 F7 **Lilliesleaf** Border
13 H5 **Limpley Stoke** Wilts
30 F3 **Lincoln** Lincs
37 G5 **Lindale** Cumb
10 C4 **Lingfield** Surrey
46 A3 **Linlithgow** W Loth
16 D3 **Linton** Cambs
10 F4 **Linton** Kent
9 H3 **Liphook** Hants
3 H4 **Liskeard** Cnwll
9 H3 **Liss** Hants
31 G2 **Lissington** Lincs
24 F4 **Litcham** Norfk
14 C7 **Litchfield** Hants
16 D3 **Little Abington** Cambs
15 K3 **Little Berkhamsted** Herts
23 H3 **Little Brickhill** M Keyn
30 F7 **Little Bytham** Lincs
17 J5 **Little Clacton** Essex
15 G3 **Little Gaddesden** Herts
36 F3 **Little Langdale** Cumb
21 H2 **Little Stretton** Shrops
4 E5 **Little Torrington** Devon
25 G3 **Little Walsingham** Norfk
33 H5 **Littleborough** Rochdl
9 K5 **Littlehampton** W Susx
24 D6 **Littleport** Cambs
32 C7 **Liverpool** Lpool
46 B3 **Livingston** W Loth
2 D8 **Lizard** Cnwll
26 C5 **Llanaelhaearn** Gwynd
27 K6 **Llanarmon Dyffryn Ceiriog** Wrexhm
19 H4 **Llanarthne** Carmth
26 E6 **Llanbedr** Gwynd
27 K4 **Llanbedr-Dyffryn-Clwyd** Denbgs
26 C6 **Llanbedrog** Gwynd
26 E4 **Llanberis** Gwynd
20 F3 **Llanbister** Powys
20 D1 **Llanbrynmair** Powys
19 H5 **Llanddarog** Carmth
27 H6 **Llandderfel** Gwynd
27 H3 **Llanddulas** Conwy
27 K5 **Llandegla** Denbgs
19 J4 **Llandeilo** Carmth
20 E2 **Llandinam** Powys
18 E4 **Llandissilio** Pembks
19 K3 **Llandovery** Carmth
20 B2 **Llandre** Cerdgn
27 J6 **Llandrillo** Denbgs
20 E4 **Llandrindod Wells** Powys
27 L7 **Llandrinio** Powys
27 G2 **Llandudno** Conwy
26 D4 **Llandwrog** Gwynd
19 J5 **Llandybie** Carmth

19 G3 **Llandysul** Cerdgn
19 H6 **Llanelli** Carmth
26 D2 **Llanerchymedd** IOA
27 J8 **Llanerfyl** Powys
26 C2 **Llanfachraeth** IOA
27 J8 **Llanfair Caereinion** Powys
27 J4 **Llanfair Dyffryn Clwyd** Denbgs
26 D3 **Llanfair P G** IOA
27 H3 **Llanfair Talhaiarn** Conwy
21 G3 **Llanfair Waterdine** Shrops
26 F3 **Llanfairfechan** Conwy
20 A3 **Llanfarian** Cerdgn
27 K7 **Llanfyllin** Powys
27 H8 **Llangadfan** Powys
19 K4 **Llangadog** Carmth
20 D5 **Llangammarch Wells** Powys
27 K7 **Llangedwyn** Powys
26 D3 **Llangefni** IOA
17 J7 **Llangeinor** Brdgnd
19 G3 **Llangeler** Carmth
19 G6 **Llangennith** Swans
27 G3 **Llangernyw** Conwy
26 E2 **Llangoed** IOA
27 K5 **Llangollen** Denbgs
20 F7 **Llangors** Powys
18 F2 **Llangranog** Cerdgn
20 D3 **Llangurig** Powys
20 F7 **Llangynidr** Powys
27 J7 **Llangynog** Powys
20 E7 **Llanhamlach** Powys
12 B3 **Llanharan** Rhondd
20 D2 **Llanidloes** Powys
20 B3 **Llanilar** Cerdgn
26 E3 **Llanllechid** Gwynd
27 H3 **Llannefydd** Conwy
27 J7 **Llanrhaeadr-ym-Mochnant** Powys
19 H6 **Llanrhidian** Swans
20 A4 **Llanrhystud** Cerdgn
26 E4 **Llanrug** Gwynd
27 G4 **Llanrwst** Conwy
27 G3 **Llansanffraid Glan Conwy** Conwy
27 H3 **Llansannan** Conwy
19 H1 **Llansantffraid** Cerdgn
27 K7 **Llansantffraid-ym-Mechain** Powys
19 J3 **Llansawel** Carmth
19 K3 **Llansteffan** Carmth
21 G7 **Llanthony** Mons
12 B3 **Llantrisant** Rhondd
5 J1 **Llantwit Major** V Glam
27 G6 **Llanuwchllyn** Gwynd
21 H8 **Llanvetherine** Mons
21 G7 **Llanvihangel Crucorney** Mons
27 J7 **Llanwddyn** Powys
26 D4 **Llanwnda** Gwynd
19 K3 **Llanwrda** Carmth
20 D5 **Llanwrtyd Wells** Powys
19 H2 **Llanybydder** Carmth
27 L2 **Llanymynech** Powys
26 D6 **Llanystumdwy** Gwynd
27 L4 **Llay** Wrexhm
18 F2 **Llechryd** Cerdgn
26 E8 **Llwyngwril** Gwynd
27 K6 **Llwynmawr** Wrexhm
27 L7 **Llynclys** Shrops
19 H2 **Llyswen** Powys
62 c12 **Loch Baghasdail** W Isls

62 d8 **Loch nam Madadh** W Isls
52 E3 **Lochailort** Highld
52 D6 **Lochaline** Highld
41 K4 **Locharbriggs** D & G
53 H7 **Lochawe** Ag & B
62 c12 **Lochboisdale** W Isls
52 D7 **Lochbuie** Ag & B
57 H5 **Lochcarron** Highld
52 D7 **Lochdonhead** Ag & B
50 B4 **Lochearnhead** Stirlg
49 H4 **Lochgair** Ag & B
49 G4 **Lochgilphead** Ag & B
49 K3 **Lochgoilhead** Ag & B
63 G5 **Lochinver** Highld
41 L4 **Lochmaben** D & G
62 d8 **Lochmaddy** W Isls
44 D3 **Lochranza** N Ayrs
45 G2 **Lochwinnoch** Rens
41 L4 **Lockerbie** D & G
39 H4 **Lockton** N York
25 K6 **Loddon** Norfk
38 B6 **Lofthouse** N York
39 G2 **Loftus** R & Cl
15 J5 **London** Gt Lon
15 J4 **London Colney** Herts
12 F4 **Long Ashton** N Som
30 E5 **Long Bennington** Lincs
23 G4 **Long Buckby** Nhants
22 D6 **Long Compton** Warwks
14 E3 **Long Crendon** Bucks
30 B6 **Long Eaton** Derbys
22 E4 **Long Itchington** Warwks
22 F3 **Long Lawford** Warwks
34 C2 **Long Marston** N York
17 G3 **Long Melford** Suffk
37 L7 **Long Preston** N York
25 J6 **Long Stratton** Norfk
31 K7 **Long Sutton** Lincs
12 F8 **Long Sutton** Somset
7 J1 **Longburton** Dorset
21 M7 **Longford** Gloucs
47 G4 **Longformacus** Border
43 J2 **Longframlington** Nthumb
8 B6 **Longham** Dorset
43 J3 **Longhorsley** Nthumb
47 M7 **Longhoughton** Nthumb
46 E3 **Longniddry** E Loth
21 J1 **Longnor** Shrops
29 H4 **Longnor** Staffs
32 F3 **Longridge** Lancs
45 M2 **Longridge** W Loth
61 G5 **Longside** Abers
32 D4 **Longton** Lancs
42 B5 **Longtown** Cumb
21 J2 **Longville in the Dale** Shrops
3 H5 **Looe** Cnwll
59 K3 **Lossiemouth** Moray
3 G5 **Lostwithiel** Cnwll
30 B7 **Loughborough** Leics
31 J2 **Louth** Lincs
37 M4 **Low Row** N York
30 D5 **Lowdham** Notts
54 H4 **Lower Diabaig** Highld
10 D6 **Lower Dicker** E Susx
28 E3 **Lower Peover** Ches
22 C7 **Lower Swell** Gloucs
25 M6 **Lowestoft** Suffk
36 E2 **Loweswater** Cumb
23 K3 **Lowick** Nhants
47 K5 **Lowick** Nthumb
23 H2 **Lubenham** Leics
35 J7 **Ludborough** Lincs
8 D2 **Ludgershall** Wilts

25 K4 **Ludham** Norfk
21 J3 **Ludlow** Shrops
45 H3 **Lugton** E Ayrs
21 J6 **Lugwardine** Herefs
55 J4 **Lumphanan** Abers
55 H3 **Lumsden** Abers
51 L2 **Lunan** Angus
37 H5 **Lupton** Cumb
49 L4 **Luss** Ag & B
56 C4 **Lusta** Highld
15 H2 **Luton** Luton
22 F2 **Lutterworth** Leics
65 H4 **Lybster** Highld
21 H2 **Lydbury North** Shrops
11 H6 **Lydd** Kent
3 L3 **Lydford** Devon
12 F7 **Lydford on Fosse** Somset
21 G2 **Lydham** Shrops
13 G2 **Lydney** Gloucs
7 G3 **Lyme Regis** Dorset
11 J4 **Lyminge** Kent
8 D6 **Lymington** Hants
28 E2 **Lymm** Warrtn
11 J5 **Lympne** Kent
8 D5 **Lyndhurst** Hants
13 K4 **Lyneham** Wilts
65 D5 **Lyness** Ork
12 E7 **Lyng** Somset
5 G3 **Lynmouth** Devon
4 F3 **Lynton** Devon
21 G5 **Lyonshall** Herefs
32 C4 **Lytham St Anne's** Lancs
39 H3 **Lythe** N York

M

31 K2 **Mablethorpe** Lincs
28 F3 **Macclesfield** Ches
60 E3 **Macduff** Abers
44 A5 **Machrihanish** Ag & B
20 C1 **Machynlleth** Powys
46 E3 **Macmerry** E Loth
26 F5 **Maentwrog** Gwynd
12 B2 **Maerdy** Rhondd
19 L7 **Maesteg** Brdgnd
32 D6 **Maghull** Sefton
13 H7 **Maiden Bradley** Wilts
7 J3 **Maiden Newton** Dorset
6 C5 **Maidencombe** Torbay
14 F5 **Maidenhead** W & M
10 F3 **Maidstone** Kent
41 K6 **Mainsriddle** D & G
6 A7 **Malborough** Devon
17 G6 **Maldon** Essex
37 L6 **Malham** N York
52 D2 **Mallaig** Highld
27 G8 **Mallwyd** Gwynd
13 J3 **Malmesbury** Wilts
28 C5 **Malpas** Ches
34 C7 **Maltby** Rothm
39 G6 **Malton** N York
21 L6 **Malvern Wells** Worcs
2 D7 **Manaccan** Cnwll
33 G6 **Manchester** Manch
24 C6 **Manea** Cambs
17 J4 **Manningtree** Essex
18 D6 **Manorbier** Pembks
30 B4 **Mansfield** Notts
2 E5 **Marazanvose** Cnwll
2 B7 **Marazion** Cnwll
24 B6 **March** Cambs
28 B5 **Marchwiel** Wrexhm
10 F4 **Marden** Kent
31 J4 **Mareham le Fen** Lincs
16 E6 **Margaretting** Essex
11 L2 **Margate** Kent

12 E6 **Mark** Somset
10 E5 **Mark Cross** E Susx
22 E1 **Market Bosworth** Leics
31 G8 **Market Deeping** Lincs
28 D6 **Market Drayton** Shrops
23 H2 **Market Harborough** Leics
13 K6 **Market Lavington** Wilts
35 H7 **Market Rasen** Lincs
34 F3 **Market Weighton** E R Yk
30 B8 **Markfield** Leics
30 D3 **Markham Moor** Notts
17 G5 **Marks Tey** Essex
13 G5 **Marksbury** BaNES
13 M4 **Marlborough** Wilts
18 B5 **Marloes** Pembks
14 F5 **Marlow** Bucks
7 K1 **Marnhull** Dorset
14 D2 **Marsh Gibbon** Bucks
13 H4 **Marshfield** S Glos
38 F2 **Marske-by-the-Sea** R & Cl
31 G4 **Martin** Lincs
7 J3 **Martinstown** Dorset
17 K3 **Martlesham Heath** Suffk
7 H1 **Martock** Somset
22 E4 **Marton** Warwks
3 K3 **Mary Tavy** Devon
55 K7 **Marykirk** Abers
41 K7 **Maryport** Cumb
55 L2 **Marywell** Abers
38 C5 **Masham** N York
10 E4 **Matfield** Kent
29 K4 **Matlock** Derbys
14 E7 **Mattingley** Hants
45 H5 **Mauchline** E Ayrs
60 F4 **Maud** Abers
36 d2 **Maughold** IOM
23 K6 **Maulden** Beds
2 E4 **Mawgan Porth** Cnwll
2 D7 **Mawnan Smith** Cnwll
45 G6 **Maybole** S Ayrs
10 E5 **Mayfield** E Susx
29 H5 **Mayfield** Staffs
12 F6 **Meare** Somset
29 K8 **Measham** Leics
9 G3 **Medstead** Hants
4 E6 **Meeth** Devon
27 K8 **Meifod** Powys
51 H3 **Meigle** P & K
16 C3 **Melbourn** Cambs
29 K7 **Melbourne** Derbys
27 J2 **Meliden** Denbgs
13 J5 **Melksham** Wilts
37 J6 **Melling** Lancs
42 D7 **Melmerby** Cumb
46 F6 **Melrose** Border
33 K5 **Meltham** Kirk
35 G4 **Melton** E R Yk
25 H3 **Melton Constable** Norfk
30 D7 **Melton Mowbray** Leics
57 G2 **Melvaig** Highld
64 E2 **Melvich** Highld
61 G3 **Memsie** Abers
51 J2 **Memus** Angus
26 E3 **Menai Bridge** IOA
17 J2 **Mendlesham** Suffk
14 F2 **Mentmore** Bucks
10 E2 **Meopham** Kent
13 H7 **Mere** Wilts
22 D3 **Meriden** Solhll
12 B2 **Merthyr Tydfil** Myr Td
4 E6 **Merton** Devon
34 F6 **Messingham** N Linc
25 K7 **Metfield** Suffk

51 J6 **Methil** Fife
60 F5 **Methlick** Abers
50 F4 **Methven** P & K
24 E6 **Methwold** Norfk
2 F6 **Mevagissey** Cnwll
34 B6 **Mexborough** Donc
62 f3 **Miabhig** W Isls
62 f3 **Miavaig** W Isls
8 F2 **Micheldever** Hants
37 M2 **Mickleton** Dur
22 C6 **Mickleton** Gloucs
61 d2 **Mid Yell** Shet
65 C2 **Midbea** Ork
35 G7 **Middle Rasen** Lincs
2 a2 **Middle Town** IOS
8 D3 **Middle Wallop** Hants
38 B4 **Middleham** N York
38 E2 **Middlesbrough** Middsb
22 F6 **Middleton Cheney** Nhants
34 F2 **Middleton on the Wolds** E R Yk
14 C2 **Middleton Stoney** Oxon
37 M2 **Middleton-in-Teesdale** Dur
9 J5 **Middleton-on-Sea** W Susx
28 E3 **Middlewich** Ches
12 E7 **Middlezoy** Somset
9 J4 **Midhurst** W Susx
13 G6 **Midsomer Norton** BaNES
7 J1 **Milborne Port** Somset
24 E7 **Mildenhall** Suffk
47 J6 **Milfield** Nthumb
18 C5 **Milford Haven** Pembks
8 D6 **Milford on Sea** Hants
3 K5 **Millbrook** Cnwll
7 b2 **Millbrook** Jersey
36 E5 **Millom** Cumb
44 F3 **Millport** N Ayrs
50 F6 **Milnathort** P & K
45 J1 **Milngavie** W Duns
7 K2 **Milton Abbas** Dorset
3 K3 **Milton Abbot** Devon
4 D6 **Milton Damerel** Devon
23 K5 **Milton Ernest** Beds
23 J6 **Milton Keynes** M Keyn
5 K5 **Milverton** Somset
13 J2 **Minchinhampton** Gloucs
5 J3 **Minehead** Somset
11 H2 **Minster** Kent
11 L2 **Minster** Kent
14 A3 **Minster Lovell** Oxon
28 B8 **Minsterley** Shrops
61 G4 **Mintlaw** Abers
33 K5 **Mirfield** Kirk
34 E7 **Misterton** Notts
7 H2 **Misterton** Somset
21 K7 **Mitcheldean** Gloucs
28 E2 **Mobberley** Ches
40 E6 **Mochrum** D & G
3 M5 **Modbury** Devon
41 L2 **Moffat** D & G
27 K4 **Mold** Flints
41 H3 **Moniaive** D & G
51 K4 **Monifieth** Angus
4 D5 **Monkleigh** Devon
45 G5 **Monkton** S Ayrs
21 J8 **Monmouth** Mons
6 a2 **Mont Saint** Guern
7 H1 **Montacute** Somset
28 B7 **Montford Bridge** Shrops
20 F1 **Montgomery** Powys

51 L2 **Montrose** Angus
29 H3 **Monyash** Derbys
55 K3 **Monymusk** Abers
5 G6 **Morchard Bishop** Devon
23 J1 **Morcott** Rutlnd
21 J6 **Mordiford** Herefs
47 H7 **Morebattle** Border
37 G6 **Morecambe** Lancs
7 K3 **Moreton** Dorset
22 C6 **Moreton-in-Marsh** Gloucs
6 B3 **Moretonhampstead** Devon
26 B5 **Morfa Nefyn** Gwynd
33 L4 **Morley** Leeds
43 J3 **Morpeth** Nthumb
25 G2 **Morston** Norfk
4 D3 **Mortehoe** Devon
14 D7 **Mortimer** W Berk
21 K2 **Morville** Shrops
4 B5 **Morwenstow** Cnwll
55 H3 **Mossat** Abers
59 L4 **Mosstodloch** Moray
7 H2 **Mosterton** Dorset
27 K2 **Mostyn** Flints
37 G1 **Motherby** Cumb
45 K3 **Motherwell** N Lans
14 D5 **Moulsford** Oxon
23 H4 **Moulton** Nhants
12 B2 **Mountain Ash** Rhondd
30 C7 **Mountsorrel** Leics
2 B7 **Mousehole** Cnwll
58 F5 **Moy** Highld
21 J7 **Much Birch** Herefs
16 C5 **Much Hadham** Herts
21 K6 **Much Marcle** Herefs
21 K1 **Much Wenlock** Shrops
55 M5 **Muchalls** Abers
4 E4 **Muddiford** Devon
58 D4 **Muir of Ord** Highld
51 K3 **Muirdrum** Angus
51 H4 **Muirhead** Angus
45 K5 **Muirkirk** E Ayrs
37 L4 **Muker** N York
2 D8 **Mullion** Cnwll
25 K3 **Mundesley** Norfk
24 E6 **Mundford** Norfk
42 B8 **Mungrisdale** Cumb
58 E4 **Munlochy** Highld
21 J2 **Munslow** Shrops
46 D3 **Musselburgh** E Loth
50 D5 **Muthill** P & K

N

17 K4 **Nacton** Suffk
12 F4 **Nailsea** N Som
13 J2 **Nailsworth** Gloucs
59 G4 **Nairn** Highld
19 H4 **Nantgaredig** Carmth
28 D5 **Nantwich** Ches
18 E5 **Narberth** Pembks
24 E4 **Narborough** Norfk
23 G3 **Naseby** Nhants
30 F4 **Navenby** Lincs
17 H4 **Nayland** Suffk
16 C6 **Nazeing** Essex
19 K6 **Neath** Neath
24 F5 **Necton** Norfk
17 J2 **Needham Market** Suffk
26 C5 **Nefyn** Gwynd
33 H3 **Nelson** Lancs
28 B7 **Nesscliffe** Shrops
27 L3 **Neston** Ches
12 C7 **Nether Stowey** Somset

36 E3 **Nether Wasdale** Cumb
54 D3 **Nethy Bridge** Highld
14 E5 **Nettlebed** Oxon
18 E3 **Nevern** Pembks
41 K5 **New Abbey** D & G
60 F3 **New Aberdour** Abers
8 F3 **New Alresford** Hants
31 J4 **New Bolingbroke** Lincs
25 H6 **New Buckenham** Norfk
45 J6 **New Cumnock** E Ayrs
60 F5 **New Deer** Abers
41 G4 **New Galloway** D & G
2 a1 **New Grimsby** IOS
35 G4 **New Holland** N Linc
40 C5 **New Luce** D & G
8 C6 **New Milton** Hants
60 F4 **New Pitsligo** Abers
19 G1 **New Quay** Cerdgn
20 F4 **New Radnor** Powys
11 H5 **New Romney** Kent
12 C2 **New Tredegar** Caerph
30 E4 **Newark-on-Trent** Notts
45 L2 **Newarthill** N Lans
37 L1 **Newbiggin** Dur
38 A5 **Newbiggin** N York
43 K3 **Newbiggin-by-the-Sea** Nthumb
46 A5 **Newbigging** S Lans
22 D5 **Newbold on Stour** Warwks
26 D4 **Newborough** IOA
12 C2 **Newbridge** Caerph
41 K4 **Newbridge** D & G
20 E4 **Newbridge on Wye** Powys
61 G6 **Newburgh** Abers
51 G5 **Newburgh** Fife
14 C6 **Newbury** W Berk
37 G5 **Newby Bridge** Cumb
18 F3 **Newcastle Emlyn** Carmth
43 K5 **Newcastle upon Tyne** N u Ty
28 F5 **Newcastle-under-Lyme** Staffs
42 C3 **Newcastleton** Border
21 L7 **Newent** Gloucs
18 C4 **Newgale** Pembks
10 C7 **Newhaven** E Susx
10 C6 **Newick** E Susx
2 B7 **Newlyn** Cnwll
45 L3 **Newmains** N Lans
16 E2 **Newmarket** Suffk
60 B4 **Newmill** Moray
13 G1 **Newnham** Gloucs
21 K4 **Newnham** Worcs
34 F4 **Newport** E R Yk
16 D4 **Newport** Essex
8 E6 **Newport** IOW
12 D3 **Newport** Newpt
18 D3 **Newport** Pembks
28 E7 **Newport** Wrekin
23 J6 **Newport Pagnell** M Keyn
51 J4 **Newport-on-Tay** Fife
2 E5 **Newquay** Cnwll
38 B3 **Newsham** N York
6 C5 **Newton Abbot** Devon
38 C2 **Newton Aycliffe** Dur
3 L6 **Newton Ferrers** Devon
45 J3 **Newton Mearns** E Rens
30 E3 **Newton on Trent** Lincs
29 J7 **Newton Solney** Derbys

6 C3 **Newton St Cyres** Devon
40 E5 **Newton Stewart** D & G
43 J2 **Newton-on-the-Moor** Nthumb
46 D4 **Newtongrange** Mdloth
54 B4 **Newtonmore** Highld
21 K5 **Newtown** Herefs
20 F2 **Newtown** Powys
51 H3 **Newtyle** Angus
18 D5 **Neyland** Pembks
59 G3 **Nigg** Highld
10 E6 **Ninfield** E Susx
8 F7 **Niton** IOW
31 G4 **Nocton** Lincs
47 J5 **Norham** Nthumb
34 B4 **Normanton** Wakefd
46 F2 **North Berwick** E Loth
34 F4 **North Cave** E R Yk
7 G3 **North Chideock** Dorset
35 K6 **North Cotes** Lincs
24 F3 **North Creake** Norfk
12 D8 **North Curry** Somset
34 F7 **North Dalton** E R Yk
25 G4 **North Elmham** Norfk
35 G4 **North Ferriby** E R Yk
35 H2 **North Frodingham** E R Yk
39 H6 **North Grimston** N York
9 G5 **North Hayling** Hants
30 F3 **North Hykeham** Lincs
58 F4 **North Kessock** Highld
23 G3 **North Kilworth** Leics
31 H4 **North Kyme** Lincs
23 J1 **North Luffenham** Rutlnd
5 G4 **North Molton** Devon
30 E4 **North Muskham** Notts
12 D7 **North Petherton** Somset
33 L2 **North Rigton** N York
43 K5 **North Shields** N Tyne
35 K6 **North Somercotes** Lincs
8 C2 **North Tidworth** Wilts
25 J3 **North Walsham** Norfk
8 F2 **North Waltham** Hants
16 D6 **North Weald Bassett** Essex
29 K4 **North Wingfield** Derbys
15 G2 **Northall** Bucks
38 D4 **Northallerton** N York
4 D4 **Northam** Devon
23 H4 **Northampton** Nhants
9 J3 **Northchapel** W Susx
11 G6 **Northiam** E Susx
22 C8 **Northleach** Gloucs
27 K3 **Northop** Flints
28 D3 **Northwich** Ches
24 E6 **Northwold** Norfk
39 G6 **Norton** N York
13 H5 **Norton St Philip** Somset
25 J5 **Norwich** Norfk
30 C5 **Nottingham** C Nott
22 F2 **Nuneaton** Warwks
13 H6 **Nunney** Somset
10 C5 **Nutley** E Susx

O

23 G1 **Oadby** Leics
30 E8 **Oakham** Rutlnd

13 G6 **Oakhill** Somset
23 K5 **Oakley** Beds
13 D3 **Oakley** Bucks
8 F2 **Oakley** Hants
13 L5 **Oare** Wilts
52 F7 **Oban** Ag & B
45 H5 **Ochiltree** E Ayrs
29 L6 **Ockbrook** Derbys
9 L2 **Ockley** Surrey
9 G2 **Odiham** Hants
22 B5 **Offenham** Worcs
13 M4 **Ogbourne St George** Wilts
19 L8 **Ogmore-by-Sea** V Glam
4 E7 **Okehampton** Devon
61 G4 **Old Deer** Abers
2 a1 **Old Grimsby** IOS
24 A7 **Old Hurst** Cambs
31 K5 **Old Leake** Lincs
60 D6 **Old Rayne** Abers
13 H3 **Old Sodbury** S Glos
23 H6 **Old Stratford** Nhants
2 b2 **Old Town** IOS
15 G6 **Old Windsor** W & M
33 H6 **Oldham** Oldham
60 F6 **Oldmeldrum** Abers
61 b3 **Ollaberry** Shet
30 C3 **Ollerton** Notts
23 J5 **Olney** M Keyn
21 M4 **Ombersley** Worcs
36 C3 **Onchan** IOM
53 G5 **Onich** Highld
17 L3 **Orford** Suffk
25 L4 **Ormesby St Margaret** Norfk
32 D6 **Ormskirk** Lancs
10 D2 **Orpington** Gt Lon
10 E1 **Orsett** Thurr
37 J3 **Orton** Cumb
31 G6 **Osbournby** Lincs
7 K4 **Osmington** Dorset
38 E4 **Osmotherley** N York
11 H3 **Ospringe** Kent
13 L5 **Ossett** Wakefd
38 F5 **Oswaldkirk** N York
27 L6 **Oswestry** Shrops
10 D3 **Otford** Kent
12 E7 **Othery** Somset
33 K3 **Otley** Leeds
49 H5 **Otter Ferry** Ag & B
8 E4 **Otterbourne** Hants
43 G3 **Otterburn** Nthumb
15 G7 **Ottershaw** Surrey
6 E4 **Otterton** Devon
6 E3 **Ottery St Mary** Devon
23 K2 **Oundle** Nhants
24 C5 **Outwell** Norfk
29 K7 **Overseal** Derbys
8 F2 **Overton** Hants
28 B5 **Overton** Wrexhm
8 D4 **Ower** Hants
14 C3 **Oxford** Oxon
10 C3 **Oxted** Surrey
30 C5 **Oxton** Notts
19 H7 **Oxwich** Swans

P

23 H7 **Padbury** Bucks
10 E4 **Paddock Wood** Kent
33 G4 **Padiham** Lancs
2 F4 **Padstow** Cnwll
6 C5 **Paignton** Torbay
22 F3 **Pailton** Warwks
13 J1 **Painswick** Gloucs
45 H2 **Paisley** Rens
41 J6 **Palnackie** D & G
21 G7 **Pandy** Mons
14 D6 **Pangbourne** W Berk

33 L2 **Pannal** N York
20 E3 **Pant-y-dwr** Powys
16 B2 **Papworth Everard** Cambs
4 F3 **Parracombe** Devon
13 G3 **Patchway** S Glos
38 B6 **Pateley Bridge** N York
45 H6 **Patna** E Ayrs
35 J4 **Patrington** E R Yk
37 G2 **Patterdale** Cumb
23 G5 **Pattishall** Nhants
10 C7 **Peacehaven** E Susx
13 H5 **Peasedown St John** BaNES
17 L1 **Peasenhall** Suffk
11 G6 **Peasmarsh** E Susx
46 C5 **Peebles** Border
36 b3 **Peel** IOM
3 H5 **Pelynt** Cnwll
19 G6 **Pembrey** Carmth
21 H4 **Pembridge** Herefs
18 D6 **Pembroke** Pembks
18 D6 **Pembroke Dock** Pembks
10 E4 **Pembury** Kent
27 J7 **Pen-y-bont-fawr** Powys
18 E6 **Penally** Pembks
12 C4 **Penarth** V Glam
12 A3 **Pencoed** Brdgnd
21 J7 **Pencraig** Herefs
18 F5 **Pendine** Carmth
21 L6 **Pendock** Worcs
3 G3 **Pendoggett** Cnwll
12 C2 **Pengam** Caerph
46 C4 **Penicuik** Mdloth
33 L6 **Penistone** Barns
29 G7 **Penkridge** Staffs
27 G5 **Penmachno** Conwy
26 F3 **Penmaenmawr** Conwy
20 B1 **Pennal** Gwynd
60 F3 **Pennan** Abers
41 J3 **Penpont** D & G
26 E6 **Penrhyndeudraeth** Gwynd
42 D8 **Penrith** Cumb
2 E7 **Penryn** Cnwll
13 G5 **Pensford** BaNES
10 D4 **Penshurst** Kent
2 F6 **Pentewan** Cnwll
26 D3 **Pentraeth** IOA
27 G5 **Pentrefoelas** Conwy
20 F4 **Penybont** Powys
26 D4 **Penygroes** Gwynd
2 B7 **Penzance** Cnwll
2 D5 **Perranporth** Cnwll
22 A5 **Pershore** Worcs
50 F4 **Perth** P & K
22 M1 **Peterborough** C Pete
21 H6 **Peterchurch** Herefs
55 L4 **Peterculter** C Aber
61 H5 **Peterhead** Abers
43 L7 **Peterlee** Dur
9 H4 **Petersfield** Hants
5 J5 **Petton** Devon
9 J4 **Petworth** W Susx
10 E7 **Pevensey** E Susx
13 L5 **Pewsey** Wilts
39 G5 **Pickering** N York
38 C2 **Piercebridge** Darltn
65 c1 **Pierowall** Ork
3 J4 **Pillaton** Cnwll
22 D5 **Pillerton Priors** Warks
32 D3 **Pilling** Lancs
31 H7 **Pinchbeck** Lincs
40 C3 **Pinwherry** S Ayrs
29 L4 **Pinxton** Derbys
15 G7 **Pirbright** Surrey
60 E6 **Pitcaple** Abers

50 E2 **Pitlochry** P & K
60 F6 **Pitmedden** Abers
51 K6 **Pittenweem** Fife
30 B4 **Pleasley** Derbys
57 H6 **Plockton** Highld
11 G4 **Pluckley** Kent
10 C6 **Plumpton** E Susx
30 C6 **Plumtree** Notts
3 K5 **Plymouth** C Plym
3 L5 **Plympton** C Plym
34 E2 **Pocklington** E R Yk
3 J5 **Polbathic** Cnwll
10 D7 **Polegate** E Susx
50 E8 **Polmont** Falk
3 H5 **Polperro** Cnwll
3 G5 **Polruan** Cnwll
2 F3 **Polzeath** Cnwll
19 K6 **Pontardawe** Neath
19 J6 **Pontarddulais** Swans
34 B5 **Pontefract** Wakefd
43 J4 **Ponteland** Nthumb
20 C3 **Ponterwyd** Cerdgn
28 B8 **Pontesbury** Shrops
12 C2 **Pontlianfraith** Caerph
19 K1 **Pontrhydfendigaid** Cerdgn
21 H7 **Pontrilas** Herefs
19 H5 **Pontyates** Carmth
19 H5 **Pontyberem** Carmth
12 D2 **Pontypool** Torfn
12 B3 **Pontypridd** Rhondd
33 L3 **Pool** Leeds
8 A6 **Poole** Poole
57 H2 **Poolewe** Highld
37 H2 **Pooley Bridge** Cumb
5 H3 **Porlock** Somset
5 H3 **Porlock Weir** Somset
52 F6 **Port Appin** Ag & B
48 D6 **Port Askaig** Ag & B
49 J6 **Port Bannatyne** Ag & B
42 A5 **Port Carlisle** Cumb
48 B7 **Port Charlotte** Ag & B
19 H7 **Port Einon** Swans
48 C8 **Port Ellen** Ag & B
36 a4 **Port Erin** IOM
49 L5 **Port Glasgow** Inver
57 G3 **Port Henderson** Highld
2 F3 **Port Isaac** Cnwll
40 C7 **Port Logan** D & G
62 i1 **Port Nis** W Isls
50 B6 **Port of Menteith** Stirlg
62 i1 **Port of Ness** W Isls
36 a4 **Port St Mary** IOM
19 K7 **Port Talbot** Neath
40 E7 **Port William** D & G
49 H6 **Portavadie** Ag & B
8 F5 **Portchester** Hants
7 J3 **Portesham** Dorset
60 B3 **Portgordon** Moray
12 B3 **Porth** Rhondd
19 L8 **Porthcawl** Brdgnd
2 E4 **Porthcothan** Cnwll
2 A8 **Porthcurno** Cnwll
2 C7 **Porthleven** Cnwll
26 E6 **Porthmadog** Gwynd
2 D6 **Porthtowan** Cnwll
36 F2 **Portinscale** Cumb
12 F4 **Portishead** N Som
60 C3 **Portknockie** Moray
55 M5 **Portlethen** Abers
2 F6 **Portloe** Cnwll
59 H2 **Portmahomack** Highld
53 G6 **Portnacroish** Ag & B
48 A7 **Portnahaven** Ag & B
40 B6 **Portpatrick** D & G
2 C6 **Portreath** Cnwll
56 E5 **Portree** Highld
2 E7 **Portscatho** Cnwll

64 E2 **Portskerra** Highld
10 B7 **Portslade-by-Sea** Br & H
9 G5 **Portsmouth** C Port
60 D3 **Portsoy** Abers
3 M3 **Postbridge** Devon
14 E4 **Postcombe** Oxon
13 K5 **Potterne** Wilts
16 B3 **Potters Bar** Herts
16 B3 **Potton** Beds
32 C3 **Poulton-le-Fylde** Lancs
47 K7 **Powburn** Nthumb
21 M5 **Powick** Worcs
28 F2 **Poynton** Ches
2 C7 **Praa Sands** Cnwll
28 C6 **Prees** Shrops
28 C6 **Prees Green** Shrops
32 D3 **Preesall** Lancs
28 E5 **Prenteg** Gwynd
27 J2 **Prestatyn** Denbgs
28 F3 **Prestbury** Ches
21 G4 **Presteigne** Powys
47 H4 **Preston** Border
32 E4 **Preston** Lancs
2 F2 **Preston Candover** Hants
22 F5 **Preston Capes** Nhants
46 E3 **Prestonpans** E Loth
33 G6 **Prestwich** Bury
45 G5 **Prestwick** S Ayrs
12 F6 **Priddy** Somset
14 F4 **Princes Risborough** Bucks
22 E3 **Princethorpe** Warwks
3 L4 **Princetown** Devon
41 L7 **Prospect** Cumb
43 H1 **Prudhoe** Nthumb
13 H4 **Pucklechurch** S Glos
7 K3 **Puddletown** Dorset
33 G4 **Pudsey** Leeds
9 K4 **Pulborough** W Susx
28 B4 **Pulford** Ches
25 J7 **Pulham St Mary** Norfk
19 J3 **Pumsaint** Carmth
10 D1 **Purfleet** Thurr
13 L3 **Purton** Wilts
19 H6 **Pwll** Carmth
26 C6 **Pwllheli** Gwynd
10 B6 **Pyecombe** W Susx
19 L7 **Pyle** Brdgnd

21 L2 **Quatt** Shrops
27 L3 **Queensferry** Flints
16 D4 **Quendon** Essex

5 H5 **Rackenford** Devon
25 J4 **Rackheath** Norfk
30 C6 **Radcliffe on Trent** Notts
15 H4 **Radlett** Herts
13 G5 **Radstock** BaNES
16 E4 **Radwinter** Essex
12 C4 **Radyr** Cardif
59 J4 **Rafford** Moray
12 E1 **Raglan** Mons
10 D1 **Rainham** Gt Lon
14 A6 **Rampside** Cumb
14 A6 **Ramsbury** Wilts
24 A7 **Ramsey** Cambs
36 c2 **Ramsey** IOM
11 L2 **Ramsgate** Kent

38 B6 **Ramsgill** N York
53 L5 **Rannoch Station** P & K
65 c2 **Rapness** Ork
61 G3 **Rathen** Abers
23 K3 **Raunds** Nhants
36 E4 **Ravenglass** Cumb
39 J3 **Ravenscar** N York
37 K3 **Ravenstonedale** Cumb
34 B7 **Rawmarsh** Rothm
33 G4 **Rawtenstall** Lancs
16 F7 **Rayleigh** Essex
14 E6 **Reading** Readg
64 F2 **Reay** Highld
11 K2 **Reculver** Kent
18 F5 **Red Roses** Carmth
43 K4 **Red Row** Nthumb
26 D2 **Red Wharf Bay** IOA
15 H3 **Redbourn** Herts
12 F1 **Redbrook** Gloucs
28 C5 **Redbrook** Wrexhm
38 F2 **Redcar** R & Cl
22 B4 **Redditch** Worcs
25 G7 **Redgrave** Suffk
12 F5 **Redhill** N Som
10 B4 **Redhill** Surrey
30 E6 **Redmile** Leics
28 B6 **Rednal** Shrops
2 D6 **Redruth** Cnwll
25 L5 **Reedham** Norfk
25 H4 **Reepham** Norfk
10 B4 **Reigate** Surrey
39 K5 **Reighton** N York
30 C7 **Rempstone** Notts
45 H2 **Renfrew** Rens
42 D7 **Renwick** Cumb
29 K6 **Repton** Derbys
19 L6 **Resolven** Neath
30 D2 **Retford** Notts
19 H7 **Reynoldston** Swans
20 D4 **Rhayader** Powys
63 H3 **Rhiconich** Highld
5 J2 **Rhoose** V Glam
27 G2 **Rhos-on-Sea** Conwy
27 L5 **Rhoslianerchrugog** Wrexhm
26 C3 **Rhosneigr** IOA
19 G7 **Rhossili** Swans
49 L5 **Rhu** Ag & B
27 J3 **Rhuddlan** Denbgs
26 E4 **Rhyd-Ddu** Gwynd
19 G2 **Rhydowen** Cerdgn
27 H2 **Rhyl** Denbgs
12 C1 **Rhymney** Caerph
21 J4 **Richards Castle** Herefs
15 J6 **Richmond** Gt Lon
38 B3 **Richmond** N York
15 H4 **Rickmansworth** Herts
43 H5 **Riding Mill** Nthumb
43 G4 **Ridsdale** Nthumb
39 H5 **Rillington** N York
41 G6 **Ringford** D & G
10 C6 **Ringmer** E Susx
8 C5 **Ringwood** Hants
29 K5 **Ripley** Derbys
38 C7 **Ripley** N York
15 H7 **Ripley** Surrey
38 D6 **Ripon** N York
21 M6 **Ripple** Worcs
33 J5 **Ripponden** Calder
12 D3 **Risca** Caerph
31 H6 **Risegate** Lincs
23 K4 **Riseley** Beds
14 E7 **Riseley** Wokham
29 L6 **Risley** Derbys
32 F7 **Risley** Warrtn
23 H5 **Roade** Nhants
46 E7 **Roberton** Border
45 M5 **Roberton** S Lans

10 F6 **Robertsbridge** E Susx
18 E5 **Robeston Wathen** Pembks
39 J3 **Robin Hood's Bay** N York
29 H6 **Rocester** Staffs
18 C4 **Roch** Pembks
33 H5 **Rochdale** Rochdl
2 F5 **Roche** Cnwll
10 F2 **Rochester** Medway
42 F3 **Rochester** Nthumb
17 G7 **Rochford** Essex
2 F3 **Rock** Cnwll
42 B5 **Rockcliffe** Cumb
41 J6 **Rockcliffe** D & G
23 J2 **Rockingham** Nhants
9 H4 **Rogate** W Susx
12 D3 **Rogerstone** Newpt
25 L4 **Rollesby** Norfk
29 J6 **Rolleston** Staffs
11 G5 **Rolvenden** Kent
37 M2 **Romaldkirk** Dur
46 C5 **Romanno Bridge** Border
16 D7 **Romford** Gt Lon
8 D4 **Romsey** Hants
43 G7 **Rookhope** Dur
9 G3 **Ropley** Hants
39 G4 **Rosedale Abbey** N York
63 K7 **Rosehall** Highld
61 G3 **Rosehearty** Abers
58 F4 **Rosemarkie** Highld
46 D4 **Rosewell** Mdloth
21 K7 **Ross-on-Wye** Herefs
28 B4 **Rossett** Wrexhm
46 B2 **Rosyth** Fife
43 H2 **Rothbury** Nthumb
10 D5 **Rotherfield** E Susx
34 B7 **Rotherham** Rothm
59 L4 **Rothes** Moray
49 J6 **Rothesay** Ag & B
33 M4 **Rothwell** Leeds
23 H3 **Rothwell** Nhants
10 C7 **Rottingdean** Br & H
25 J3 **Roughton** Norfk
9 G5 **Rowland's Castle** Hants
43 J6 **Rowland's Gill** Gatesd
29 J3 **Rowsley** Derbys
47 G6 **Roxburgh** Border
16 E6 **Roxwell** Essex
34 A5 **Royston** Barns
16 C4 **Royston** Herts
7 c1 **Rozel** Jersey
27 L5 **Ruabon** Wrexhm
30 C6 **Ruddington** Notts
9 K3 **Rudgwick** W Susx
59 K6 **Rudston** E R Yk
32 D5 **Rufford** Lancs
22 F3 **Rugby** Warwks
29 G7 **Rugeley** Staffs
50 F6 **Rumbling Bridge** P & K
28 C2 **Runcorn** Halton
39 H2 **Runswick** N York
23 K4 **Rushden** Nhants
38 C1 **Rushyford** Dur
9 K5 **Ruskington** Lincs
9 K5 **Rustington** W Susx
39 H3 **Ruswarp** N York
45 J2 **Rutherglen** S Lans
27 J4 **Ruthin** Denbgs
28 B7 **Ruyton-XI-Towns** Shrops
37 G3 **Rydal** Cumb
8 F6 **Ryde** IOW
11 G6 **Rye** E Susx

S

44 B5	**Saddell** Ag & B	
16 D4	**Saffron Walden** Essex	
47 J3	**St Abbs** Border	
2 D5	**St Agnes** Cnwll	
15 H3	**St Albans** Herts	
6 a2	**St Andrew** Guern	
51 K5	**St Andrews** Fife	
12 F2	**St Arvans** Mons	
27 J3	**St Asaph** Denbgs	
5 J1	**St Athan** V Glam	
7 b2	**St Aubin** Jersey	
2 F5	**St Austell** Cnwll	
36 D3	**St Bees** Cumb	
3 G5	**St Blazey** Cnwll	
46 F6	**St Boswells** Border	
7 a2	**St Brelade** Jersey	
7 a2	**St Brelade's Bay** Jersey	
12 F2	**St Briavels** Gloucs	
2 A7	**St Buryan** Cnwll	
49 J3	**St Catherines** Ag & B	
18 F5	**St Clears** Carmth	
3 H4	**St Cleer** Cnwll	
7 c2	**St Clement** Jersey	
2 F4	**St Columb Major** Cnwll	
61 H3	**St Combs** Abers	
55 K7	**St Cyrus** Abers	
18 B4	**St David's** Pembks	
2 D6	**St Day** Cnwll	
18 E2	**St Dogmaels** Cerdgn	
61 H4	**St Fergus** Abers	
50 C4	**St Fillans** P & K	
18 E6	**St Florence** Pembks	
9 G6	**St Helens** IOW	
32 E7	**St Helens** St Hel	
7 b2	**St Helier** Jersey	
24 A8	**St Ives** Cambs	
2 B6	**St Ives** Cnwll	
7 b1	**St John** Jersey	
36 b3	**St John's** IOM	
43 G7	**St John's Chapel** Dur	
41 G4	**St John's Town of Dalry** D & G	
36 c2	**St Jude's** IOM	
2 A7	**St Just** Cnwll	
2 E7	**St Just-in-Roseland** Cnwll	
2 E8	**St Keverne** Cnwll	
3 H5	**St Keyne** Cnwll	
8 F7	**St Lawrence** IOW	
7 b1	**St Lawrence** Jersey	
11 L4	**St Margaret's at Cliffe** Kent	
65 c5	**St Margaret's Hope** Ork	
36 b3	**St Marks** IOM	
6 b2	**St Martin** Guern	
7 c1	**St Martin** Jersey	
7 b1	**St Mary** Jersey	
65 c4	**St Mary's** IOS	
11 J5	**St Mary's Bay** Kent	
2 E7	**St Mawes** Cnwll	
2 E4	**St Mawgan** Cnwll	
51 K6	**St Monans** Fife	
23 M4	**St Neots** Cambs	
17 J5	**St Osyth** Essex	
7 a1	**St Ouen** Jersey	
21 J7	**St Owens Cross** Herefs	
7 b1	**St Peter** Jersey	
6 b2	**St Peter Port** Guern	
6 a2	**St Peter's** Guern	
6 b1	**St Sampson** Guern	
6 a2	**St Saviour** Guern	
7 b2	**St Saviour** Jersey	
2 F5	**St Stephen** Cnwll	
3 G3	**St Tudy** Cnwll	
6 B7	**Salcombe** Devon	
33 G7	**Sale** Traffd	
52 D6	**Salen** Ag & B	
52 E4	**Salen** Highld	
10 B4	**Salfords** Surrey	
50 F7	**Saline** Fife	
8 C3	**Salisbury** Wilts	
3 K5	**Saltash** Cnwll	
38 F2	**Saltburn-by-the-Sea** R & Cl	
44 F4	**Saltcoats** N Ayrs	
35 K7	**Saltfleet** Lincs	
5 K5	**Sampford Arundel** Somset	
5 J3	**Sampford Brett** Somset	
48 B6	**Sanaigmore** Ag & B	
28 E4	**Sandbach** Ches	
49 K5	**Sandbank** Ag & B	
14 C4	**Sandford-on-Thames** Oxon	
61 G3	**Sandhaven** Abers	
40 C6	**Sandhead** D & G	
14 F7	**Sandhurst** Br For	
61 a5	**Sandness** Shet	
29 G6	**Sandon** Staffs	
8 F7	**Sandown** IOW	
15 J3	**Sandridge** Herts	
39 H3	**Sandsend** N York	
11 L3	**Sandwich** Kent	
61 c7	**Sandwick** Shet	
23 L5	**Sandy** Beds	
45 L6	**Sanquhar** D & G	
26 B6	**Sarn** Gwynd	
21 H5	**Sarnesfield** Herefs	
11 K2	**Sarre** Kent	
34 E7	**Saundby** Notts	
18 E5	**Saundersfoot** Pembks	
4 D4	**Saunton** Devon	
16 D5	**Sawbridgeworth** Herts	
16 D3	**Sawston** Cambs	
23 L3	**Sawtry** Cambs	
30 E7	**Saxby** Leics	
30 E3	**Saxilby** Lincs	
17 L2	**Saxmundham** Suffk	
25 H3	**Saxthorpe** Norfk	
48 C4	**Scalasaig** Ag & B	
39 J4	**Scalby** N York	
61 c6	**Scalloway** Shet	
31 J3	**Scamblesby** Lincs	
39 K4	**Scarborough** N York	
48 b2	**Scarinish** Ag & B	
34 F6	**Scawby** N Linc	
25 H7	**Scole** Norfk	
51 G4	**Scone** P & K	
56 E6	**Sconser** Highld	
38 C3	**Scotch Corner** N York	
34 F6	**Scotter** Lincs	
38 B4	**Scotton** N York	
25 G5	**Scoulton** Norfk	
63 G4	**Scourie** Highld	
65 G2	**Scrabster** Highld	
34 F5	**Scunthorpe** N Linc	
25 L3	**Sea Palling** Norfk	
10 D7	**Seaford** E Susx	
43 L6	**Seaham** Dur	
47 L6	**Seahouses** Nthumb	
10 D3	**Seal** Kent	
39 J5	**Seamer** N York	
36 D3	**Seascale** Cumb	
36 F4	**Seathwaite** Cumb	
6 F3	**Seaton** Devon	
43 K4	**Seaton Delaval** Nthumb	
38 F4	**Seave Green** N York	
9 G6	**Seaview** IOW	
37 J4	**Sedbergh** Cumb	
22 B6	**Sedgeberrow** Worcs	
30 E6	**Sedgebrook** Lincs	
38 D1	**Sedgefield** Dur	
10 F6	**Sedlescombe** E Susx	
13 K5	**Seend** Wilts	
28 F7	**Seighford** Staffs	
9 G3	**Selborne** Hants	
34 D4	**Selby** N York	
46 E6	**Selkirk** Border	
11 J4	**Sellindge** Kent	
9 H6	**Selsey** W Susx	
29 L4	**Selston** Notts	
15 G7	**Send** Surrey	
12 C3	**Senghenydd** Caerph	
2 A7	**Sennen** Cnwll	
20 D7	**Sennybridge** Powys	
24 D4	**Setchey** Norfk	
37 L6	**Settle** N York	
19 L5	**Seven Sisters** Neath	
10 D3	**Sevenoaks** Kent	
J8	**Shaftesbury** Dorset	
16 F4	**Shalford** Essex	
K2	**Shalford** Surrey	
49 K5	**Shandon** Ag & B	
8 F7	**Shanklin** IOW	
37 H2	**Shap** Cumb	
29 L6	**Shardlow** Derbys	
23 K4	**Sharnbrook** Beds	
13 G2	**Sharpness** Gloucs	
3 L4	**Shaugh Prior** Devon	
28 E5	**Shavington** Ches	
28 C7	**Shawbury** Shrops	
4 D6	**Shebbear** Devon	
4 E6	**Sheepwash** Devon	
11 G2	**Sheerness** Kent	
29 K2	**Sheffield** Sheff	
23 L6	**Shefford** Beds	
16 C3	**Shepreth** Cambs	
30 B7	**Shepshed** Leics	
13 G6	**Shepton Mallet** Somset	
7 J1	**Sherborne** Dorset	
39 J5	**Sherburn** N York	
34 C4	**Sherburn in Elmet** N York	
14 D7	**Sherfield on Loddon** Hants	
38 F6	**Sheriff Hutton** N York	
25 H2	**Sheringham** Norfk	
57 J7	**Shiel Bridge** Highld	
57 H4	**Shieldaig** Highld	
28 E8	**Shifnal** Shrops	
38 C2	**Shildon** Dur	
14 D4	**Shillingford** Oxon	
7 L2	**Shillingstone** Dorset	
14 E6	**Shinfield** Wokham	
25 G5	**Shipdham** Norfk	
14 E6	**Shiplake** Oxon	
33 K3	**Shipley** Brad	
22 D6	**Shipston on Stour** Warwks	
38 E7	**Shipton** N York	
34 E3	**Shiptonthorpe** E R Yk	
9 L5	**Shoreham-by-Sea** W Susx	
8 E7	**Shorwell** IOW	
17 K4	**Shotley** Suffk	
17 L3	**Shottisham** Suffk	
45 L2	**Shotts** N Lans	
28 C8	**Shrewsbury** Shrops	
13 L6	**Shrewton** Wilts	
13 M3	**Shrivenham** Oxon	
22 A7	**Shurdington** Gloucs	
6 F3	**Shute** Devon	
31 J5	**Sibsey** Lincs	
22 E1	**Sibson** Leics	
6 E3	**Sidmouth** Devon	
14 D7	**Silchester** Hants	
30 C7	**Sileby** Leics	
31 G5	**Silk Willoughby** Lincs	
41 L6	**Silloth** Cumb	
23 L6	**Silsoe** Beds	
16 F5	**Silver End** Essex	
37 H5	**Silverdale** Lancs	
23 G6	**Silverstone** Nhants	
5 H6	**Silverton** Devon	
42 F4	**Simonburn** Nthumb	
5 G4	**Simonsbath** Somset	
38 D5	**Sinderby** N York	
9 J4	**Singleton** W Susx	
10 F4	**Sissinghurst** Kent	
11 G3	**Sittingbourne** Kent	
8 A4	**Sixpenny Handley** Dorset	
31 L4	**Skegness** Lincs	
30 F3	**Skellingthorpe** Lincs	
32 D6	**Skelmersdale** Lancs	
49 K6	**Skelmorlie** N Ayrs	
42 C7	**Skelton** Cumb	
38 F2	**Skelton** R & Cl	
21 H7	**Skenfrith** Mons	
64 C2	**Skerray** Highld	
44 C3	**Skipness** Ag & B	
35 H2	**Skipsea** E R Yk	
33 J2	**Skipton** N York	
46 B6	**Skirling** Border	
42 D8	**Skirwith** Cumb	
32 F2	**Slaidburn** Lancs	
43 G6	**Slaley** Nthumb	
45 L1	**Slamannan** Falk	
6 B7	**Slapton** Devon	
31 G5	**Sleaford** Lincs	
39 J6	**Sledmere** E R Yk	
39 H5	**Sleights** N York	
39 G5	**Slingsby** N York	
15 G5	**Slough** Slough	
47 G6	**Smailholm** Border	
11 G4	**Smarden** Kent	
42 C5	**Smithfield** Cumb	
39 J5	**Snainton** N York	
17 L2	**Snape** Suffk	
24 E3	**Snettisham** Norfk	
10 E3	**Snodland** Kent	
24 D7	**Soham** Cambs	
22 C3	**Solihull** Solhll	
18 B4	**Solva** Pembks	
24 B7	**Somersham** Cambs	
12 F7	**Somerton** Somset	
9 L5	**Sompting** W Susx	
14 E5	**Sonning** Wokham	
14 E5	**Sonning Common** Oxon	
40 E6	**Sorbie** D & G	
37 K3	**Soulby** Cumb	
22 F6	**Souldern** Oxon	
23 K4	**Souldrop** Beds	
3 L2	**Sourton** Devon	
16 F8	**South Benfleet** Essex	
6 A5	**South Brent** Devon	
34 F4	**South Cave** E R Yk	
34 B5	**South Elmsall** Wakefd	
9 H4	**South Harting** W Susx	
9 G5	**South Hayling** Hants	
9 L2	**South Holmwood** Surrey	
31 H5	**South Kyme** Lincs	
15 J4	**South Mimms** Herts	
4 F5	**South Molton** Devon	
29 L4	**South Normanton** Derbys	
16 E8	**South Ockendon** Thurr	
7 G1	**South Petherton** Somset	
46 B3	**South Queensferry** C Edin	
24 F4	**South Raynham** Norfk	
43 L5	**South Shields** S Tyne	
38 C6	**South Stainley** N York	
25 K4	**South Waisham** Norfk	
30 F7	**South Witham** Lincs	
16 F7	**South Woodham Ferrers** Essex	
3 M2	**South Zeal** Devon	
22 E4	**Southam** Warwks	
8 E5	**Southampton** C Sotn	

10 D4 **Southborough** Kent	23 J7 **Stewkley** Bucks	33 G7 **Stretford** Traffd
44 B6 **Southend** Ag & B	9 L5 **Steyning** W Susx	24 C7 **Stretham** Cambs
17 G8 **Southend-on-Sea** Sthend	4 D5 **Stibb Cross** Devon	30 F7 **Stretton** Rutlnd
24 D6 **Southery** Norfk	31 J4 **Stickford** Lincs	61 G4 **Strichen** Abers
17 H7 **Southminster** Essex	31 J4 **Stickney** Lincs	57 H5 **Stromeferry** Highld
14 B4 **Southmoor** Oxon	25 G2 **Stiffkey** Norfk	65 D4 **Stromness** Ork
32 C5 **Southport** Sefton	38 F6 **Stillington** N York	49 M3 **Stronachlachar** Stirlg
25 J3 **Southrepps** Norfk	23 L2 **Stilton** Cambs	49 K5 **Strone** Ag & B
9 G6 **Southsea** C Port	50 D7 **Stirling** Stirlg	52 F5 **Strontian** Highld
30 D4 **Southwell** Notts	16 E7 **Stock** Essex	10 F2 **Strood** Medway
9 G5 **Southwick** Hants	8 D3 **Stockbridge** Hants	13 J2 **Stroud** Gloucs
10 B7 **Southwick** W Susx	33 H7 **Stockport** Stockp	58 C5 **Struy** Highld
25 L7 **Southwold** Suffk	33 L6 **Stocksbridge** Sheff	61 G5 **Stuartfield** Abers
38 D5 **Sowerby** N York	38 E2 **Stockton-on-Tees** S on T	8 B7 **Studland** Dorset
31 H7 **Spalding** Lincs	12 C6 **Stogursey** Somset	22 B4 **Studley** Warwks
13 G8 **Sparkford** Somset	16 F3 **Stoke by Clare** Suffk	7 K1 **Sturminster Newton** Dorset
8 E3 **Sparsholt** Hants	6 C3 **Stoke Canon** Devon	11 J3 **Sturry** Kent
53 J3 **Spean Bridge** Highld	24 E5 **Stoke Ferry** Norfk	30 E2 **Sturton by Stow** Lincs
43 K7 **Spennymoor** Dur	6 C6 **Stoke Fleming** Devon	29 H6 **Sudbury** Derbys
7 L2 **Spetisbury** Dorset	6 C6 **Stoke Gabriel** Devon	17 G3 **Sudbury** Suffk
60 B3 **Spey Bay** Moray	23 J5 **Stoke Goldington** M Keyn	36 C2 **Sulby** IOM
31 K3 **Spilsby** Lincs	21 K5 **Stoke Lacy** Herefs	2 E5 **Summercourt** Cnwll
58 F1 **Spinningdale** Highld	14 F3 **Stoke Mandeville** Bucks	15 H6 **Sunbury** Surrey
65 H3 **Spittal** Highld	15 G5 **Stoke Poges** Bucks	43 L6 **Sunderland** Sundld
54 E7 **Spittal of Glenshee** P & K	17 H4 **Stoke-by-Nayland** Suffk	31 H6 **Surfleet** Lincs
25 J4 **Spixworth** Norfk	28 F5 **Stoke-on-Trent** C Stke	31 J6 **Sutterton** Lincs
34 A2 **Spofforth** N York		24 C7 **Sutton** Cambs
41 H5 **Springholm** D & G	14 E4 **Stokenchurch** Bucks	10 B2 **Sutton** Gt Lon
35 H4 **Sproatley** E R Yk	38 F6 **Stokesley** N York	13 K4 **Sutton Benger** Wilts
14 D4 **Stadhampton** Oxon	28 F6 **Stone** Staffs	24 C4 **Sutton Bridge** Lincs
62 c11 **Stadhlaigearraidh** W Isls	55 L5 **Stonehaven** Abers	22 C2 **Sutton Coldfield** Birm
56 E3 **Staffin** Highld	13 H2 **Stonehouse** Gloucs	14 C4 **Sutton Courtenay** Oxon
28 F7 **Stafford** Staffs	45 K3 **Stonehouse** S Lans	31 L2 **Sutton on Sea** Lincs
38 B2 **Staindrop** Dur	40 B6 **Stoneykirk** D & G	30 E3 **Sutton on Trent** Notts
15 G6 **Staines** Surrey	14 E5 **Stonor** Oxon	8 E2 **Sutton Scotney** Hants
37 L6 **Stainforth** N York	62 h3 **Stornoway** W Isls	10 F4 **Sutton Valence** Kent
39 G2 **Staithes** N York	10 B7 **Storrington** W Susx	38 F6 **Sutton-on-the-Forest** N York
25 K4 **Stalham** Norfk	16 A4 **Stotfold** Beds	29 K7 **Swadlincote** Derbys
31 G8 **Stamford** Lincs	22 A5 **Stoulton** Worcs	24 F5 **Swaffham** Norfk
39 G7 **Stamford Bridge** E R Yk	21 M3 **Stourbridge** Dudley	13 H4 **Swainswick** BaNES
43 H5 **Stamfordham** Nthumb	7 L2 **Stourpaine** Dorset	22 E6 **Swalcliffe** Oxon
41 K7 **Standingstone** Cumb	21 L3 **Stourport-on-Severn** Worcs	35 H6 **Swallow** Lincs
32 E5 **Standish** Wigan	21 M2 **Stourton** Staffs	14 E7 **Swallowfield** Wokham
16 C5 **Standon** Herts	4 E5 **Stow** Border	8 B7 **Swanage** Dorset
14 B4 **Stanford in the Vale** Oxon	16 D2 **Stow-cum-Quy** Cambs	10 D2 **Swanley** Kent
10 E1 **Stanford le Hope** Thurr	22 C7 **Stow-on-the-Wold** Gloucs	19 J6 **Swansea** Swans
43 G7 **Stanhope** Dur	17 K4 **Stowmarket** Suffk	29 K4 **Swanwick** Derbys
43 J6 **Stanley** Dur	55 K5 **Strachan** Abers	8 F5 **Swanwick** Hants
50 F4 **Stanley** P & K	49 J3 **Strachur** Ag & B	31 G6 **Swaton** Lincs
43 J4 **Stannington** Nthumb	25 J7 **Stradbroke** Suffk	16 C1 **Swavesey** Cambs
16 D5 **Stansted Mountfitchet** Essex	16 F3 **Stradishall** Suffk	8 D6 **Sway** Hants
25 G7 **Stanton** Suffk	24 D5 **Stradsett** Norfk	13 J3 **Swindon** Swindn
13 J4 **Stanton St Quintin** Wilts	45 G7 **Straiton** S Ayrs	23 K4 **Swineshead** Beds
22 B6 **Stanway** Gloucs	40 B5 **Stranraer** D & G	31 H5 **Swineshead** Lincs
6 F1 **Staple Fitzpaine** Somset	14 E7 **Stratfield Turgis** Hants	22 F3 **Swinford** Leics
30 B6 **Stapleford** Notts	17 L2 **Stratford St Andrew** Suffk	47 H5 **Swinton** Border
10 F4 **Staplehurst** Kent	22 C5 **Stratford-upon-Avon** Warwks	34 B6 **Swinton** Rothm
37 M5 **Starbotton** N York	45 K4 **Strathaven** S Lans	24 F3 **Syderstone** Norfk
37 H4 **Staveley** Cumb	50 B8 **Strathblane** Stirlg	61 d4 **Symbister** Shet
29 L3 **Staveley** Derbys	63 G7 **Strathcanaird** Highld	45 G5 **Symington** S Ayrs
22 F4 **Staverton** Nhants	55 G3 **Strathdon** Abers	46 A6 **Symington** S Lans
39 J5 **Staxton** N York	51 G5 **Strathmiglo** Fife	21 J8 **Symonds Yat** Herefs
17 G6 **Steeple** Essex	58 D4 **Strathpeffer** Highld	23 G4 **Syresham** Nhants
22 F7 **Steeple Aston** Oxon	64 E2 **Strathy** Highld	30 C8 **Syston** Leics
16 E3 **Steeple Bumpstead** Essex	50 B5 **Strathyre** Stirlg	
50 D8 **Stenhousemuir** Falk	4 B6 **Stratton** Cnwll	
62 h3 **Steornabhagh** W Isls	13 G6 **Stratton-on-the-Fosse** Somset	
16 B5 **Stevenage** Herts	14 D5 **Streatley** W Berk	34 B3 **Tadcaster** N York
44 F4 **Stevenston** N Ayrs	12 F7 **Street** Somset	14 D7 **Tadley** Hants
14 C5 **Steventon** Oxon	38 F4 **Strensall** York	59 G2 **Tain** Highld
45 H3 **Stewarton** E Ayrs	6 C6 **Strete** Devon	62 f6 **Tairbeart** W Isls
		20 B2 **Tal-y-bont** Cerdgn
		26 F3 **Tal-y-Bont** Conwy

26 E7 **Tal-y-bont** Gwynd	
27 G3 **Tal-y-Cafn** Conwy	
19 G2 **Talgarreg** Cerdgn	
20 F6 **Talgarth** Powys	
42 D6 **Talkin** Cumb	
57 J3 **Talladale** Highld	
19 J3 **Talley** Carmth	
64 C2 **Talmine** Highld	
26 E6 **Talsarnau** Gwynd	
22 C1 **Tamworth** Staffs	
18 F2 **Tan-y-groes** Cerdgn	
51 J2 **Tannadice** Angus	
14 F5 **Taplow** Bucks	
49 G6 **Tarbert** Ag & B	
62 f6 **Tarbert** W Isls	
49 L3 **Tarbet** Ag & B	
45 H5 **Tarbolton** S Ayrs	
55 H4 **Tarland** Abers	
32 D5 **Tarleton** Lancs	
28 C4 **Tarporley** Ches	
7 M2 **Tarrant Hinton** Dorset	
56 F7 **Tarskavaig** Highld	
60 F6 **Tarves** Abers	
28 C3 **Tarvin** Ches	
31 H4 **Tattershall** Lincs	
12 D8 **Taunton** Somset	
25 H4 **Taverham** Norfk	
3 K4 **Tavistock** Devon	
44 B3 **Tayinloan** Ag & B	
22 D8 **Taynton** Oxon	
53 G7 **Taynuilt** Ag & B	
51 J4 **Tayport** Fife	
48 F5 **Tayvallich** Ag & B	
37 J3 **Tebay** Cumb	
6 B3 **Tedburn St Mary** Devon	
22 A6 **Teddington** Gloucs	
6 C4 **Teignmouth** Devon	
28 E8 **Telford** Wrekin	
46 D4 **Temple** Mdloth	
19 H2 **Temple Bar** Cerdgn	
37 J1 **Temple Sowerby** Cumb	
13 H8 **Templecombe** Somset	
23 L5 **Tempsford** Beds	
21 K4 **Tenbury Wells** Worcs	
18 E6 **Tenby** Pembks	
11 G5 **Tenterden** Kent	
28 D6 **Ternhill** Shrops	
24 C4 **Terrington St Clement** Norfk	
13 J3 **Tetbury** Gloucs	
31 J3 **Tetford** Lincs	
35 J6 **Tetney** Lincs	
14 E4 **Tetsworth** Oxon	
42 C2 **Teviothead** Border	
21 M6 **Tewkesbury** Gloucs	
11 H3 **Teynham** Kent	
14 E3 **Thame** Oxon	
14 C6 **Thatcham** W Berk	
16 E4 **Thaxted** Essex	
36 c2 **The Bungalow** IOM	
14 D6 **Theale** W Berk	
17 M2 **Theberton** Suffk	
24 F7 **Thetford** Norfk	
17 G7 **Theydon Bois** Essex	
38 D5 **Thirsk** N York	
13 G3 **Thornbury** S Glos	
34 D5 **Thorne** Donc	
24 A5 **Thorney** C Pete	
24 E2 **Thornham** Norfk	
41 J3 **Thornhill** D & G	
50 C6 **Thornhill** Stirlg	
43 L7 **Thornley** Dur	
51 H6 **Thornton** Fife	
39 H5 **Thornton le Dale** N York	
38 C5 **Thornton Watlass** N York	

38 D5 **Thornton-le-Street** N York
25 J5 **Thorpe End** Norfk
17 J5 **Thorpe-le-Soken** Essex
17 M2 **Thorpeness** Suffk
17 J5 **Thorrington** Essex
23 K3 **Thrapston** Nhants
20 F6 **Three Cocks** Powys
31 G6 **Threekingham** Lincs
36 F2 **Threlkeld** Cumb
37 M6 **Threshfield** N York
43 H2 **Thropton** Nthumb
65 J4 **Thrumster** Highld
34 C7 **Thurcroft** Rothm
6 A7 **Thurlestone** Devon
34 B6 **Thurnscoe** Barns
42 B6 **Thursby** Cumb
65 G2 **Thurso** Highld
27 K2 **Thurstaston** Wirral
17 G2 **Thurston** Suffk
37 L4 **Thwaite** N York
29 L4 **Tibshelf** Derbys
10 E5 **Ticehurst** E Susx
34 C7 **Tickhill** Donc
29 K7 **Ticknall** Derbys
29 H3 **Tideswell** Derbys
62 c8 **Tigh a Ghearraidh** W Isls
62 c8 **Tigharry** W Isls
10 E2 **Tilbury** Thurr
9 J2 **Tilford** Surrey
50 E6 **Tillicoultry** Clacks
13 K6 **Tilshead** Wilts
28 C6 **Tilstock** Shrops
30 D8 **Tilton on the Hill** Leics
3 G3 **Tintagel** Cnwll
12 F2 **Tintern Parva** Mons
17 G5 **Tiptree** Essex
13 K7 **Tisbury** Wilts
29 J5 **Tissington** Derbys
28 F6 **Tittensor** Staffs
5 H6 **Tiverton** Devon
52 C5 **Tobermory** Ag & B
23 K7 **Toddington** Beds
51 J3 **Todhills** Angus
42 B5 **Todhills** Cumb
33 H4 **Todmorden** Calder
61 c3 **Toft** Shet
38 B1 **Toft Hill** Dur
62 i2 **Tolastadh** W Isls
7 M1 **Tollard Royal** Wilts
17 H6 **Tollesbury** Essex
17 G6 **Tolleshunt D'Arcy** Essex
7 K3 **Tolpuddle** Dorset
62 i2 **Tolsta** W Isls
59 G6 **Tomatin** Highld
54 F3 **Tomintoul** Moray
59 K6 **Tomnavoulin** Moray
10 E4 **Tonbridge** Kent
64 C3 **Tongue** Highld
12 B3 **Tonypandy** Rhondd
12 B3 **Tonyrefail** Rhondd
38 D5 **Topcliffe** N York
6 D3 **Topsham** Devon
44 C5 **Torbeg** N Ayrs
6 B7 **Torcross** Devon
58 E4 **Tore** Highld
30 E3 **Torksey** Lincs
46 A3 **Torphichen** W Loth
55 J4 **Torphins** Abers
3 K5 **Torpoint** Cnwll
6 C5 **Torquay** Torbay
45 J1 **Torrance** E Duns
57 H4 **Torridon** Highld
56 F7 **Torrin** Highld
46 B2 **Torryburn** Fife
41 K4 **Torthorwald** D & G
36 F4 **Torver** Cumb
8 D6 **Totland** IOW
6 B5 **Totnes** Devon
8 D4 **Totton** Hants
43 J7 **Tow Law** Dur
23 G5 **Towcester** Nhants
47 H6 **Town Yetholm** Border
46 D6 **Traquair** Border
33 H3 **Trawden** Lancs
26 F6 **Trawsfynydd** Gwynd
26 B2 **Trearddur Bay** IOA
20 D7 **Trecastle** Powys
12 C1 **Tredegar** Blae G
2 A8 **Treen** Cnwll
27 G4 **Trefriw** Conwy
19 J1 **Tregaron** Cerdgn
2 F6 **Tregony** Cnwll
19 M6 **Treherbert** Rhondd
12 F2 **Trelleck** Mons
26 E5 **Tremadog** Gwynd
43 L7 **Trimdon** Dur
25 J3 **Trimingham** Norfk
14 F3 **Tring** Herts
7 b1 **Trinity** Jersey
45 G5 **Troon** S Ayrs
9 H4 **Trotton** W Susx
37 G3 **Troutbeck** Cumb
13 J5 **Trowbridge** Wilts
2 E6 **Truro** Cnwll
23 H1 **Tugby** Leics
50 D7 **Tullibody** Clacks
50 D2 **Tummel Bridge** P & K
10 E4 **Tunbridge Wells** Kent
17 L2 **Tunstall** Suffk
44 F7 **Turnberry** S Ayrs
29 K5 **Turnditch** Derbys
10 B5 **Turner's Hill** W Susx
60 E4 **Turriff** Abers
23 K5 **Turvey** Beds
29 J6 **Tutbury** Staffs
30 D3 **Tuxford** Notts
22 E1 **Twycross** Leics
8 E4 **Twyford** Hants
14 E6 **Twyford** Wokham
41 G6 **Twynholm** D & G
53 K7 **Tyndrum** Stirlg
43 L5 **Tynemouth** N Tyne
6 F2 **Tytherleigh** Devon
20 A1 **Tywyn** Gwynd

U

10 D6 **Uckfield** E Susx
5 J6 **Uffculme** Devon
14 A5 **Uffington** Oxon
6 A6 **Ugborough** Devon
56 D3 **Uig** Highld
35 H5 **Ulceby** N Linc
42 A7 **Uldale** Cumb
63 G7 **Ullapool** Highld
22 C4 **Ullenhall** Warwks
36 E4 **Ulpha** Cumb
61 c3 **Ulsta** Shet
36 F5 **Ulverston** Cumb
4 F5 **Umberleigh** Devon
63 H4 **Unapool** Highld
13 L5 **Upavon** Wilts
6 F3 **Uplyme** Devon
6 E2 **Upottery** Devon
9 L5 **Upper Beeding** W Susx
23 K2 **Upper Benefield** Nhants
30 D6 **Upper Broughton** Notts
51 J6 **Upper Largo** Fife
21 K8 **Upper Lydbrook** Gloucs
29 G5 **Upper Tean** Staffs
23 J1 **Uppingham** Rutlnd
11 K3 **Upstreet** Kent
3 J4 **Upton Cross** Cnwll
22 A5 **Upton Snodsbury** Worcs
21 M6 **Upton upon Severn** Worcs
13 K5 **Urchfont** Wilts
12 E2 **Usk** Mons
29 H6 **Uttoxeter** Staffs
15 H5 **Uxbridge** Gt Lon
61 d2 **Uyeasound** Shet

V

6 b1 **Vale** Guern
8 F7 **Ventnor** IOW
8 B5 **Verwood** Dorset
61 c4 **Vidlin** Shet
15 G6 **Virginia Water** Surrey
61 c4 **Voe** Shet

W

14 E3 **Waddesdon** Bucks
33 G3 **Waddington** Lancs
30 F4 **Waddington** Lincs
2 F4 **Wadebridge** Cnwll
15 K3 **Wadesmill** Herts
10 E5 **Wadhurst** E Susx
31 K4 **Wainfleet All Saints** Lincs
33 M5 **Wakefield** Wakefd
25 L7 **Walberswick** Suffk
28 E5 **Walgherton** Ches
46 D6 **Walkerburn** Border
16 B5 **Walkern** Herts
35 G3 **Walkington** E R Yk
32 C7 **Wallasey** Wirral
14 D5 **Wallingford** Oxon
61 b5 **Walls** Shet
22 B1 **Walsall** Wsall
35 J6 **Waltham** NE Lin
16 C7 **Waltham Abbey** Essex
30 E7 **Waltham on the Wolds** Leics
21 G4 **Walton** Powys
12 F7 **Walton** Somset
17 K5 **Walton on the Naze** Essex
15 H6 **Walton-on-Thames** Surrey
45 L6 **Wanlockhead** D & G
23 L1 **Wansford** C Pete
13 H6 **Wanstrow** Somset
14 B5 **Wantage** Oxon
24 A7 **Warboys** Cambs
37 K2 **Warcop** Cumb
29 J3 **Wardlow** Derbys
15 K3 **Ware** Herts
7 L3 **Wareham** Dorset
47 L6 **Warenford** Nthumb
14 E6 **Wargrave** Wokham
47 H6 **Wark** Nthumb
42 F4 **Wark** Nthumb
43 K2 **Warkworth** Nthumb
22 E5 **Warmington** Warwks
13 J6 **Warminster** Wilts
10 B5 **Warninglid** W Susx
32 F7 **Warrington** Warrtn
8 E5 **Warsash** Hants
29 H4 **Warslow** Staffs
30 C3 **Warsop** Notts
32 D4 **Warton** Lancs
42 C6 **Warwick** Cumb
22 D4 **Warwick** Warwks
65 b2 **Wasbister** Ork
36 E3 **Wasdale Head** Cumb
30 F3 **Washingborough** Lincs
43 K6 **Washington** Sundld
5 J3 **Watchet** Somset
37 H4 **Watchgate** Cumb
16 D2 **Waterbeach** Cambs
42 A4 **Waterbeck** D & G
29 H5 **Waterhouses** Staffs
9 G5 **Waterlooville** Hants
37 G2 **Watermillock** Cumb
15 H4 **Watford** Herts
23 G4 **Watford** Nhants
34 B6 **Wath upon Dearne** Rothm
14 E4 **Watlington** Oxon
65 H3 **Watten** Highld
24 F5 **Watton** Norfk
15 K2 **Watton-at-Stone** Herts
42 F7 **Wearhead** Dur
24 F4 **Weasenham All Saints** Norfk
28 D3 **Weaverham** Ches
12 E6 **Wedmore** Somset
23 G4 **Weedon** Nhants
4 B7 **Week St Mary** Cnwll
50 D2 **Weem** P & K
30 F4 **Welbourn** Lincs
22 D5 **Wellesbourne** Warwks
23 J4 **Wellingborough** Nhants
5 K5 **Wellington** Somset
28 D8 **Wellington** Wrekin
12 F6 **Wells** Somset
24 F2 **Wells-next-the-sea** Norfk
24 C6 **Welney** Norfk
28 B6 **Welshampton** Shrops
27 K8 **Welshpool** Powys
23 G4 **Welton** Nhants
15 J3 **Welwyn** Herts
15 J3 **Welwyn Garden City** Herts
28 C6 **Wem** Shrops
15 J5 **Wembley** Gt Lon
3 L6 **Wembury** Devon
14 F3 **Wendover** Bucks
38 B4 **Wensley** N York
34 B5 **Wentbridge** Wakefd
21 H5 **Weobley** Herefs
24 D5 **Wereham** Norfk
38 B2 **West Auckland** Dur
7 H3 **West Bay** Dorset
7 H3 **West Bexington** Dorset
24 E4 **West Bilney** Norfk
30 C6 **West Bridgford** Notts
22 B2 **West Bromwich** Sandw
46 A4 **West Calder** W Loth
9 K4 **West Chiltington** W Susx
27 L7 **West Felton** Shrops
10 D7 **West Firle** E Susx
23 G3 **West Haddon** Nhants
10 C5 **West Hoathly** W Susx
15 H8 **West Horsley** Surrey
12 D6 **West Huntspill** Somset
44 F3 **West Kilbride** N Ayrs
27 K2 **West Kirby** Wirral
13 K6 **West Lavington** Wilts
46 C5 **West Linton** Border
7 L4 **West Lulworth** Dorset
24 D4 **West Lynn** Norfk
10 E3 **West Malling** Kent
21 L5 **West Malvern** Worcs
9 G4 **West Meon** Hants
17 H6 **West Mersea** Essex
8 B5 **West Moors** Dorset
24 E3 **West Newton** Norfk

12 F7 **West Pennard** Somset
2 D5 **West Pentire** Cnwll
38 D3 **West Rounton** N York
25 J2 **West Runton** Norfk
61 C3 **West Sandwick** Shet
9 H6 **West Wittering** W Susx
38 A4 **West Witton** N York
43 G3 **West Woodburn** Nthumb
28 B8 **Westbury** Shrops
13 J6 **Westbury** Wilts
9 L2 **Westcott** Surrey
10 C3 **Westerham** Kent
10 F6 **Westfield** E Susx
41 L7 **Westnewton** Cumb
16 B4 **Weston** Herts
29 G6 **Weston** Staffs
28 E7 **Weston Heath** Shrops
22 C6 **Weston Subedge** Gloucs
14 C3 **Weston-on-the-Green** Oxon
12 D5 **Weston-Super-Mare** N Som
28 D6 **Weston-under-Redcastle** Shrops
13 J3 **Westonbirt** Gloucs
47 G5 **Westruther** Border
4 D4 **Westward Ho!** Devon
42 C6 **Wetheral** Cumb
34 B3 **Wetherby** Leeds
39 J7 **Wetwang** E R Yk
25 H2 **Weybourne** Norfk
15 H7 **Weybridge** Surrey
8 D2 **Weyhill** Hants
7 J4 **Weymouth** Dorset
29 G2 **Whaley Bridge** Derbys
33 G3 **Whalley** Lancs
31 J7 **Whaplode** Lincs
31 J7 **Whaplode Drove** Lincs
40 E6 **Whauphill** D & G
15 J3 **Wheathampstead** Herts
14 D3 **Wheatley** Oxon
5 H4 **Wheddon Cross** Somset
17 G2 **Whepstead** Suffk
8 E2 **Wherwell** Hants
43 J5 **Whickham** Gatesd
6 A3 **Whiddon Down** Devon
6 D3 **Whimple** Devon
15 G3 **Whipsnade** Beds
46 A4 **Whitburn** W Loth
39 H3 **Whitby** N York
14 E2 **Whitchurch** Bucks
8 E2 **Whitchurch** Hants
21 J8 **Whitchurch** Herefs
28 C5 **Whitchurch** Shrops
21 J6 **White Stone** Herefs
58 D7 **Whitebridge** Highld
36 D2 **Whitehaven** Cumb
60 D3 **Whitehills** Abers
49 G6 **Whitehouse** Ag & B
46 F7 **Whitekirk** E Loth
32 F3 **Whitewell** Lancs
40 E7 **Whithorn** D & G
44 E5 **Whiting Bay** N Ayrs
18 E5 **Whitland** Carmth
43 K5 **Whitley Bay** N Tyne
43 G6 **Whitley Chapel** Nthumb
13 H1 **Whitminster** Gloucs
11 J2 **Whitstable** Kent
27 L6 **Whittington** Shrops
23 G6 **Whittlebury** Nhants
24 A6 **Whittlesey** Cambs
21 G4 **Whitton** Powys

30 B3 **Whitwell** Derbys
15 J2 **Whitwell** Herts
65 J3 **Wick** Highld
16 F7 **Wickford** Essex
8 F5 **Wickham** Hants
17 K2 **Wickham Market** Suffk
13 H3 **Wickwar** S Glos
43 K3 **Widdrington** Nthumb
6 A4 **Widecombe in the Moor** Devon
3 J5 **Widegates** Cnwll
4 B6 **Widemouth Bay** Cnwll
16 C5 **Widford** Herts
30 C6 **Widmerpool** Notts
28 C2 **Widnes** Halton
32 E6 **Wigan** Wigan
24 D4 **Wiggenhall St Germans** Norfk
23 G1 **Wigston** Leics
42 A6 **Wigton** Cumb
40 E6 **Wigtown** D & G
34 D2 **Wilberfoss** E R Yk
23 J4 **Wilby** Nhants
5 J6 **Willand** Devon
24 B8 **Willingham** Cambs
22 C4 **Wilmcote** Warwks
6 F2 **Wilmington** Devon
28 F7 **Wilmslow** Ches
46 A4 **Wilsontown** S Lans
23 L6 **Wilstead** Beds
13 L7 **Wilton** Wilts
24 B6 **Wimblington** Cambs
8 A5 **Wimborne Minster** Dorset
13 H7 **Wincanton** Somset
22 B7 **Winchcombe** Gloucs
11 G6 **Winchelsea** E Susx
8 E3 **Winchester** Hants
37 G4 **Windermere** Cumb
15 G6 **Windsor** W & M
14 F2 **Wing** Bucks
43 L7 **Wingate** Dur
11 K3 **Wingham** Kent
11 K4 **Wingmore** Kent
14 F6 **Winkfield** Br For
4 F6 **Winkleigh** Devon
12 E5 **Winscombe** N Som
28 D3 **Winsford** Ches
5 H4 **Winsford** Somset
7 G2 **Winsham** Somset
23 H7 **Winslow** Bucks
29 J4 **Winster** Derbys
7 J3 **Winterborne Monkton** Dorset
7 L2 **Winterborne Stickland** Dorset
7 L2 **Winterborne Whitechurch** Dorset
7 J3 **Winterbourne Abbas** Dorset
13 L7 **Winterbourne Stoke** Wilts
34 F5 **Winteringham** N Linc
8 C3 **Winterslow** Wilts
34 F5 **Winterton** N Linc
23 L3 **Winwick** Cambs
29 J4 **Wirksworth** Derbys
31 K8 **Wisbech** Cambs
9 K3 **Wisborough Green** W Susx
45 L3 **Wishaw** N Lans
16 F5 **Witham** Essex
5 G6 **Witheridge** Devon
31 K2 **Withern** Lincs
35 K4 **Withernsea** E R Yk
22 B8 **Withington** Gloucs
10 D5 **Withyham** E Susx
5 H4 **Withypool** Somset
17 J3 **Witnesham** Suffk
14 B3 **Witney** Oxon

11 G5 **Wittersham** Kent
43 J8 **Witton le Wear** Dur
5 J4 **Wiveliscombe** Somset
10 C6 **Wivelsfield** E Susx
17 H5 **Wivenhoe** Essex
17 J4 **Wix** Essex
23 K6 **Woburn** Beds
15 G7 **Woking** Surrey
14 F6 **Wokingham** Wokham
18 C4 **Wolf's Castle** Pembks
23 J4 **Wollaston** Nhants
27 L8 **Wollaston** Shrops
43 H7 **Wolsingham** Dur
21 M2 **Wolverhampton** Wolves
22 E2 **Wolvey** Warwks
38 E2 **Wolviston** S on T
21 M2 **Wombourne** Staffs
34 B6 **Wombwell** Barns
14 F5 **Wooburn** Bucks
17 K3 **Woodbridge** Suffk
11 G5 **Woodchurch** Kent
13 G2 **Woodford** Gloucs
31 H4 **Woodhall Spa** Lincs
38 B2 **Woodland** Dur
14 C3 **Woodstock** Oxon
21 J4 **Woofferton** Shrops
12 F6 **Wookey Hole** Somset
7 L3 **Wool** Dorset
4 D3 **Woolacombe** Devon
47 K6 **Wooler** Nthumb
14 D6 **Woolhampton** W Berk
17 H2 **Woolpit** Suffk
28 E5 **Woore** Shrops
35 G5 **Wootton** N Linc
14 B2 **Wootton** Oxon
13 L3 **Wootton Bassett** Wilts
5 H3 **Wootton Courtenay** Somset
22 C4 **Wootton Wawen** Warwks
21 M5 **Worcester** Worcs
36 D1 **Workington** Cumb
30 C2 **Worksop** Notts
17 K1 **Worlingworth** Suffk
51 J4 **Wormit** Fife
15 G7 **Worplesdon** Surrey
7 M4 **Worth Matravers** Dorset
21 G1 **Worthen** Shrops
9 L5 **Worthing** W Susx
13 H3 **Wotton-under-Edge** Gloucs
31 G3 **Wragby** Lincs
6 A6 **Wrangaton** Devon
31 K5 **Wrangle** Lincs
35 G6 **Wrawby** N Linc
39 G5 **Wrelton** N York
25 L7 **Wrentham** Suffk
16 B3 **Wrestlingworth** Beds
27 L5 **Wrexham** Wrexhm
13 L4 **Wroughton** Swindn
8 F7 **Wroxall** IOW
28 D8 **Wroxeter** Shrops
25 K4 **Wroxham** Norfk
22 E6 **Wroxton** Oxon
23 L5 **Wybsoton** Beds
11 H4 **Wye** Kent
13 K7 **Wylye** Wilts
30 E7 **Wymondham** Leics
25 H5 **Wymondham** Norfk

6 F2 **Yarcombe** Devon
23 H5 **Yardley Gobion** Nhants
23 J5 **Yardley Hastings** Nhants
38 D3 **Yarm** S on T
8 D6 **Yarmouth** IOW
46 E6 **Yarrowford** Border
14 F7 **Yateley** Hants
12 E5 **Yatton** N Som
13 J4 **Yatton Keynell** Wilts
23 M2 **Yaxley** Cambs
33 K3 **Yeadon** Leeds
3 L5 **Yealmpton** Devon
3 L4 **Yelverton** Devon
25 K5 **Yelverton** Norfk
7 H1 **Yeovil** Somset
12 F8 **Yeovilton** Somset
50 E6 **Yetts o' Muckhart** Clacks
34 C2 **York** York
29 J4 **Youlgreave** Derbys
29 H7 **Yoxall** Staffs
17 L1 **Yoxford** Suffk
20 B3 **Ysbyty Ystwyth** Cerdgn
19 K5 **Ystalyfera** Powys
12 C2 **Ystrad Mynach** Caerph
19 K5 **Ystradgynlais** Powys

Z

13 H7 **Zeals** Wilts
2 B6 **Zennor** Cnwll

Y

26 D3 **Y Felinheli** Gwynd
27 H5 **Y Maerdy** Conwy
26 B6 **Y Rhiw** Gwynd

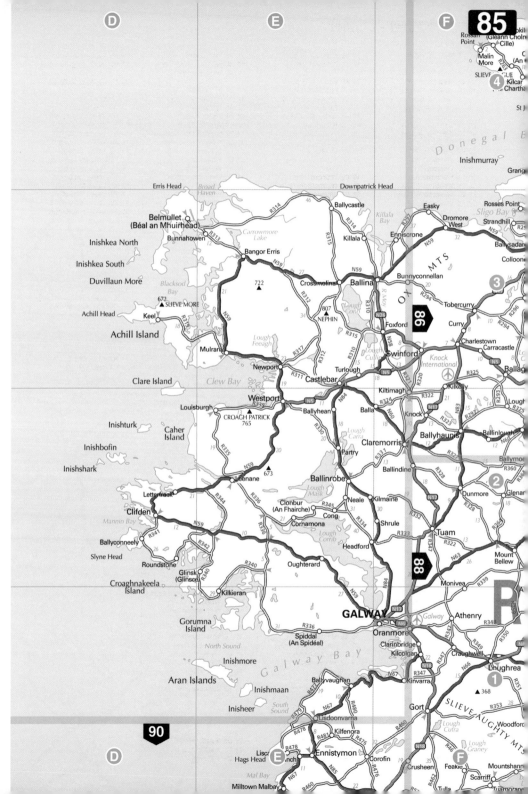

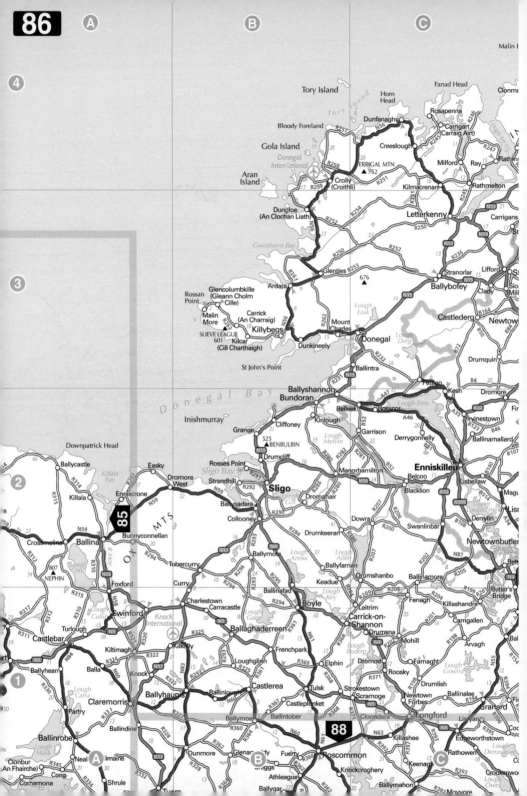

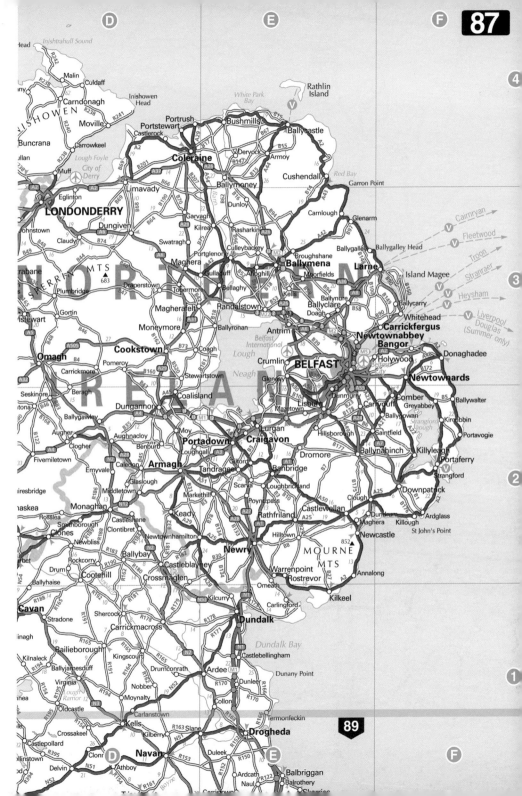

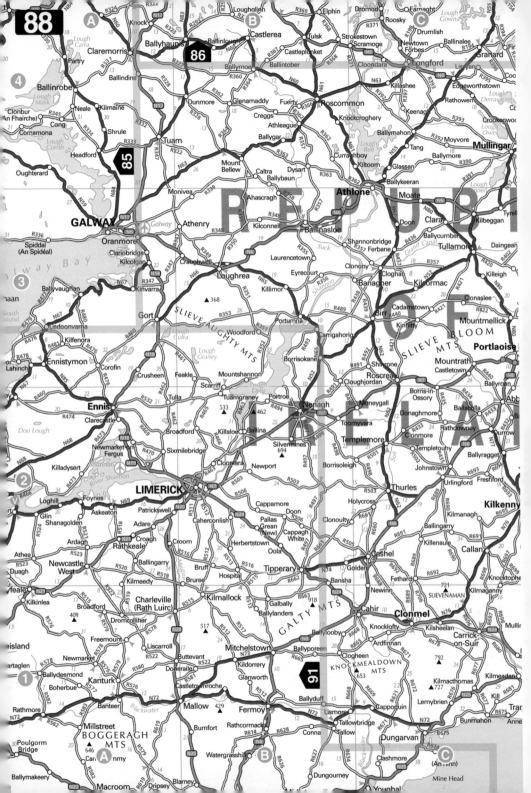

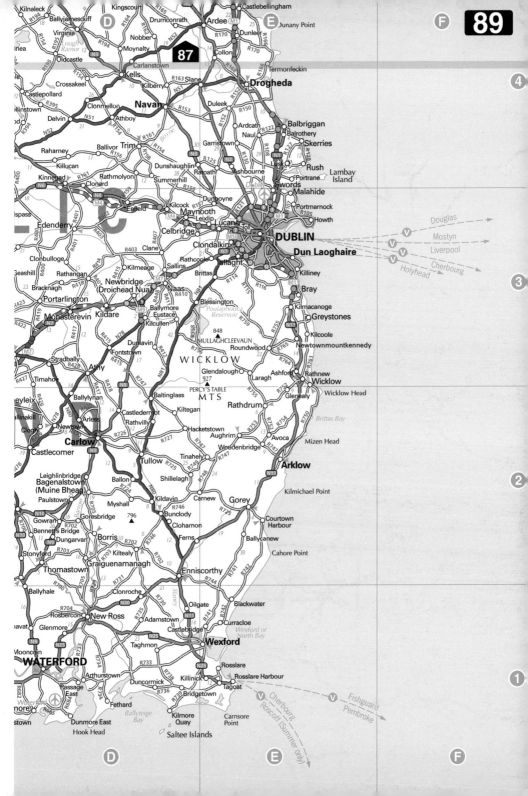

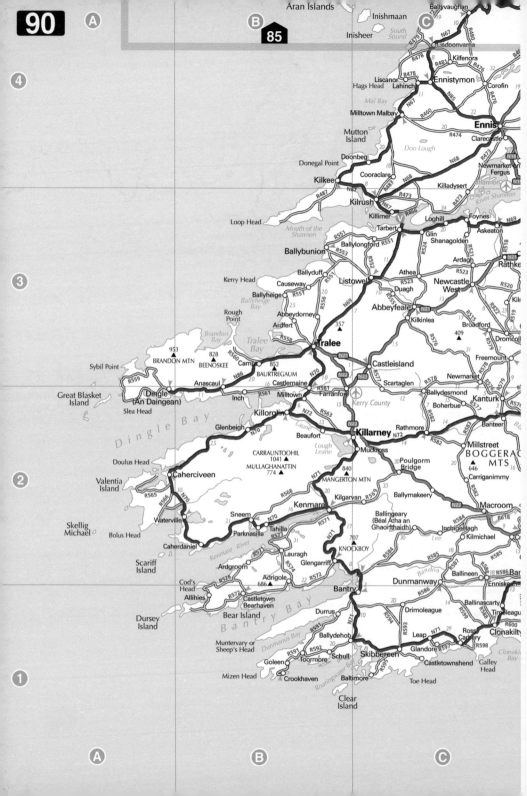

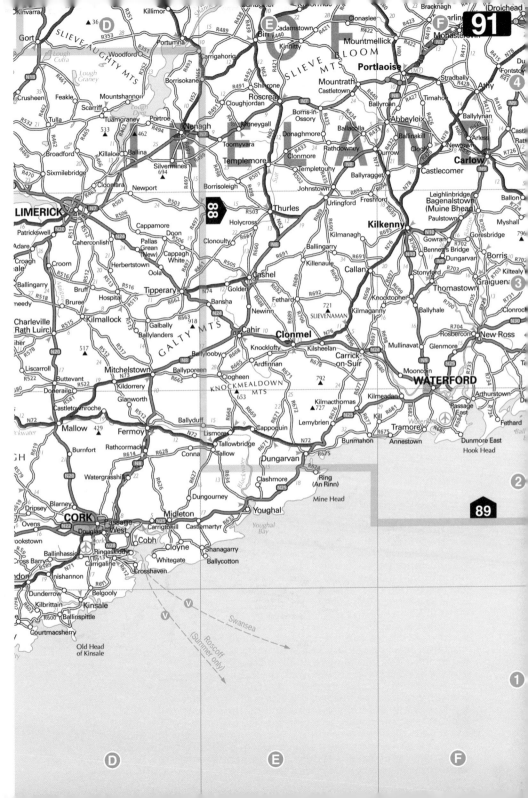

Mileage chart - Ireland

The mileage chart shows distances in miles between two towns along AA-recommended routes. Using motorways and other main roads this is normally the fastest route, though not necessarily the shortest.

Distances on the mapping are shown in miles. However, in the Republic of Ireland, distances on signposting are in kilometres

16 kilometres = 10 miles

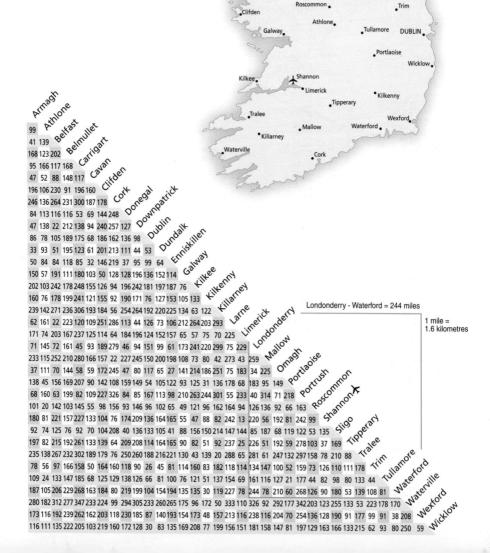

Londonderry - Waterford = 244 miles

1 mile = 1.6 kilometres

	Armagh	Athlone	Belfast	Belmullet	Carrigart	Cavan	Clifden	Cork	Donegal	Downpatrick	Dublin	Dundalk	Enniskillen	Galway	Kilkee	Kilkenny	Killarney	Larne	Limerick	Londonderry	Mallow	Omagh	Portlaoise	Portrush	Roscommon	Shannon	Sligo	Tipperary	Tralee	Trim	Tullamore	Waterford	Waterville	Wexford
Athlone	99																																	
Belfast	41	139																																
Belmullet	168	123	202																															
Carrigart	95	166	117	168																														
Cavan	47	52	88	148	117																													
Clifden	196	106	230	91	196	160																												
Cork	246	136	264	231	300	187	178																											
Donegal	84	113	116	116	53	69	144	248																										
Downpatrick	47	138	22	212	138	94	240	257	127																									
Dublin	86	78	105	189	175	68	186	162	136	98																								
Dundalk	33	93	51	195	123	61	201	213	111	44	53																							
Enniskillen	50	84	84	118	85	32	146	219	37	95	99	64																						
Galway	150	57	191	111	180	103	50	128	128	196	136	152	114																					
Kilkee	202	103	242	178	248	155	126	94	196	242	181	197	187	76																				
Kilkenny	160	76	178	199	241	121	155	92	190	171	76	127	153	105	133																			
Killarney	239	142	271	236	306	193	184	56	254	264	192	220	225	134	63	122																		
Larne	62	161	22	223	120	109	251	286	113	44	126	73	106	212	264	203	293																	
Limerick	171	74	203	167	237	125	114	64	184	196	124	152	157	65	57	75	70	225																
Londonderry	71	145	72	161	45	93	189	279	46	94	151	99	61	173	241	220	299	75	229															
Mallow	233	115	252	210	280	166	157	22	227	245	150	200	198	108	73	80	42	273	43	259														
Omagh	37	111	70	144	58	59	172	245	47	80	117	65	27	141	214	186	251	75	183	34	225													
Portlaoise	138	45	156	169	207	90	142	108	159	149	54	105	122	93	125	31	136	178	68	183	95	149												
Portrush	68	160	63	199	82	109	227	326	84	85	167	113	98	210	263	244	301	55	233	40	314	71	218											
Roscommon	101	20	142	103	145	55	98	156	93	146	96	102	65	49	121	96	162	164	94	126	136	92	66	163										
Shannon	180	81	221	157	227	133	104	76	174	209	136	164	165	55	47	88	82	242	13	220	56	192	81	242	99									
Sligo	92	74	125	76	92	70	104	208	40	136	133	105	41	88	156	150	214	147	144	85	187	68	119	122	53	135								
Tipperary	197	82	215	192	261	133	139	64	209	208	114	164	165	90	82	51	92	237	25	226	51	192	59	278	103	37	169							
Tralee	235	138	267	232	302	189	179	76	250	260	188	216	221	130	43	139	20	288	65	281	61	247	132	297	158	78	210	88						
Trim	78	56	97	166	158	50	164	160	118	90	26	45	81	114	160	83	182	118	114	134	147	100	52	159	73	126	110	111	178					
Tullamore	109	24	133	147	185	68	125	129	138	126	66	81	100	76	121	51	137	154	69	161	116	127	21	177	44	82	98	80	133	44				
Waterford	187	105	206	229	268	163	184	80	219	199	104	154	194	135	135	30	119	227	78	244	78	210	60	268	126	90	180	53	139	108	81			
Waterville	280	182	312	277	347	233	224	99	294	305	233	260	265	175	96	172	50	333	110	326	92	292	177	342	203	123	255	133	53	223	178	170		
Wexford	173	116	192	239	262	162	203	118	230	185	87	140	193	154	173	48	157	213	116	238	116	204	70	254	136	128	190	91	177	99	91	38	208	
Wicklow	116	111	135	222	205	103	219	160	172	128	30	83	135	169	208	77	199	156	151	181	158	147	81	197	129	163	166	133	215	62	93	80	250	59

A

90 B3 Abbeydorney
90 C3 Abbeyfeale
88 C2 Abbeyleix
89 D1 Adamstown
91 D5 Adare
90 B2 Adrigole
88 B3 Ahascragh
87 E3 Ahoghill
90 B1 Allihies
90 B2 Anascaul
87 E2 Annalong
88 C1 Annestown
87 E3 Antrim
90 C3 Ardagh
86 B3 Ardara
89 E4 Ardcath
87 E1 Ardee
90 B3 Ardfert
88 C1 Ardfinnan
87 F2 Ardglass
90 B2 Ardgroom
89 E2 Arklow
89 D2 Arless
87 D2 Armagh
87 E4 Armoy
89 D1 Arthurstown
86 C1 Arvagh
89 E4 Ashbourne
89 E3 Ashford
90 C3 Askeaton
89 D4 Athboy
90 C3 Athea
88 B3 Athenry
88 B4 Athleague
88 C3 Athlone
89 D3 Athy
87 D2 Augher
87 D2 Aughnacloy
89 E2 Aughrim

B

89 D2 Bagenalstown
(Muine Bheag)
87 D1 Bailieborough
89 E4 Balbriggan
85 F2 Balla
88 C2 Ballacolla
86 B1 Ballaghaderreen
85 F3 Ballina
91 D4 Ballina
86 B2 Ballinafad
86 C1 Ballinagh
88 C2 Ballinakill
86 C1 Ballinalee
86 C2 Ballinamallard
86 C2 Ballinamore
90 C1 Ballinascarty
88 B3 Ballinasloe
88 A4 Ballindine
90 C2 Ballineen
91 D3 Ballingarry
88 C2 Ballingarry
90 C2 Ballingeary
(Béal Átha an
Chaorfthaidh)
91 D2 Ballinhassig
86 B1 Ballinlough
85 E2 Ballinrobe
91 D1 Ballinspittle
86 B1 Ballintober
86 C3 Ballintra
89 D4 Ballivor
89 D2 Ballon
88 B4 Ballybaun
87 D2 Ballybay
86 C3 Ballybofey
90 B3 Ballybunion
89 E2 Ballycanew
87 F3 Ballycarry
87 E4 Ballycastle
85 E3 Ballycastle
87 E3 Ballyclare
85 D2 Ballyconneely
91 E2 Ballycotton
88 C3 Ballycumber
90 B2 Ballydehob
90 C2 Ballydesmond
90 B3 Ballyduff
91 E2 Ballyduff
86 B2 Ballyfarnan
87 E3 Ballygalley
88 B4 Ballygar
87 D2 Ballygawley
87 F2 Ballygowan
87 D1 Ballyhaise
89 D1 Ballyhale
86 B1 Ballyhaunis
85 E2 Ballyhean
90 B3 Ballyheige
87 D1 Ballyjamesduff
88 C4 Ballykeeran
91 D3 Ballylanders
90 C3 Ballylongford
88 B1 Ballylooby
89 D2 Ballylynan
88 C4 Ballymahon
90 C2 Ballymakeery
87 E3 Ballymena

88 B4 Ballymoe
87 E4 Ballymoney
88 C4 Ballymore
89 D3 Ballymore Eustace
86 B2 Ballymote
87 E2 Ballynahinch
87 E3 Ballynure
91 D3 Ballyporeen
88 C2 Ballyragget
88 C2 Ballyroan
87 E3 Ballyronan
86 B2 Ballysadare
86 B2 Ballyshannon
85 E1 Ballyvaughan
87 F2 Ballywalter
89 E4 Balrothery
90 C1 Baltimore
89 D2 Baltinglass
88 C3 Banagher
87 E2 Banbridge
91 D2 Bandon
87 F3 Bangor
85 E3 Bangor Erris
88 B2 Bansha
90 C2 Banteer
90 C1 Bantry
90 B2 Beaufort
96 C2 Belcoo
87 E3 Belfast
91 D2 Belgooly
87 E3 Bellaghy
86 C2 Belleek
85 D3 Belmullet
(Béal an Mhuirhead)
86 C2 Belturbet
87 D2 Benburb
87 D2 Bennett's Bridge
87 D2 Beragh
87 D2 Birr
86 C2 Blacklion
89 E1 Blackwater
91 D2 Blarney
89 D3 Blessington
90 C2 Boherbue
89 D2 Borris
88 C2 Borris-in-Ossory
91 E4 Borrisokane
88 C2 Borrisoleigh
86 B1 Boyle
89 D3 Bracknagh
89 E3 Bray
89 D1 Bridgetown
89 E3 Brittas
91 D4 Broadford
90 C3 Broadford
87 E3 Broughshane
91 D3 Bruff
91 D3 Bruree
89 D2 Bunclody
86 C4 Buncrana
86 B2 Bundoran
88 C1 Bunmahon
85 E3 Bunnahowen
85 F3 Bunnyconnellan
91 D2 Burnfort
87 E4 Bushmills
86 C1 Butler's Bridge
91 D3 Buttevant

C

88 C3 Cadamstown
91 D3 Caherconlish
90 B2 Caherdaniel
90 A2 Caherciveen
88 C1 Cahir
87 D2 Caledon
88 B4 Callan
88 B4 Caltra
90 B3 Camp
91 D3 Cappagh White
89 D3 Cappamore
88 C1 Cappoquin
87 D1 Carlanstown
87 E1 Carlingford
89 D2 Carlow
87 D4 Carndonagh
89 E2 Carnew
87 E3 Carnlough
86 B1 Carracastle
86 B3 Carrick
(An Charraig)
87 F3 Carrickfergus
87 D1 Carrickmacross
87 D1 Carrickmore
86 B1 Carrick-on-Shannon
88 C1 Carrick-on-Suir
91 E4 Carrigahorig
91 D2 Carrigaline
86 C1 Carrigallen
90 C2 Carriganimmy
87 D3 Carrigans
86 C4 Carrigart
(Carraig Airt)
91 D2 Carrigtohill
87 D4 Carrowkeel
87 E2 Carryduff
88 C2 Cashel
85 E3 Castlebar
87 E1 Castlebellingham
87 D2 Castleblayney
89 E1 Castlebridge

89 D2 Castlecomer
86 C3 Castlederg
89 D2 Castledermot
90 C3 Castleisland
88 C3 Castlemaine
91 E2 Castlemartyr
86 B1 Castleplunket
89 D4 Castlepollard
86 B1 Castlerea
87 D4 Castlerock
87 D2 Castleshane
88 C3 Castletown
90 B1 Castletown
Bearhaven
91 D2 Castletownroche
90 C1 Castletownshend
87 E2 Castlewellan
90 B3 Causeway
86 C1 Cavan
89 E3 Celbridge
86 B1 Charlestown
91 D3 Charleville
(Rath Luirc)
86 C3 Clady
89 D3 Clane
88 C3 Clara
90 C4 Clarecastle
85 F2 Claremorris
88 A3 Clarinbridge
91 E2 Clashmore
87 D3 Claudy
85 D2 Clifden
86 B2 Cliffoney
89 D2 Clogh
88 C3 Cloghan
88 B1 Clogheen
87 D2 Clogher
89 D2 Clohamon
90 C1 Clonakilty
89 D4 Clonard
88 C3 Clonaslee
89 D3 Clonbulloge
85 E2 Clonbur (An
Fhairche)
89 E3 Clondalkin
87 D4 Clonmany
88 C1 Clonmel
89 D4 Clonmellon
88 C2 Clonmore
88 C3 Clonony
89 D1 Clonroche
87 D2 Clontibret
86 C1 Cloondara
91 D4 Cloonlara
87 F2 Clough
88 B3 Cloughjordan
91 D2 Cloyne
87 D3 Coagh
87 D2 Coalisland
91 D2 Cobh
87 D4 Coleraine
89 D4 Collinstown
87 E1 Collon
86 B2 Collooney
87 F2 Comber
85 E2 Cong
91 D2 Conna
87 D3 Cookstown
88 C4 Coole
90 C4 Cooraclare
87 D2 Cootehill
91 D2 Cork
85 E2 Cornamona
90 C4 Corofin
91 D1 Courtmacsherry
89 E2 Courtown Harbour
87 E2 Craigavon
88 B3 Craughwell
86 C4 Creeslough
88 B4 Creggs
90 C3 Croagh
86 B4 Crolly (Croithlí)
89 D4 Crookedwood
90 B1 Crookhaven
90 C2 Crookstown
91 D3 Croom
89 D4 Crossakeel
91 D2 Cross Barry
91 D2 Crosshaven
87 D2 Crossmaglen
85 E3 Crossmolina
87 E3 Crumlin
91 D4 Crusheen
87 D4 Culdaff
87 E3 Culleybackey
89 E1 Curracloe
88 B4 Curraghboy
86 B1 Curry
87 E4 Cushendall

D

89 D3 Daingean
89 D4 Delvin
86 C2 Derrygonnelly
87 E4 Dervock
86 C2 Derrylin
90 A2 Dingle
(An Daingean)
87 E3 Doagh

87 F3 Donaghadee
88 C2 Donaghmore
86 C3 Donegal
91 D2 Doneraile
90 C4 Doon
90 C4 Doonbeg
91 D2 Douglas
87 F2 Downpatrick
86 C2 Dowra
87 D3 Draperstown
90 C1 Drimoleague
91 D2 Dripsey
89 E4 Drogheda
86 B2 Dromahair
90 C3 Dromcolliher
86 C1 Dromod
87 E2 Dromore
86 C2 Dromore
86 A2 Dromore West
87 D2 Drum
86 B2 Drumcliff
87 D1 Drumconrath
86 C2 Drumkeeran
86 C1 Drumlish
86 C3 Drumquin
86 C2 Drumshanbo
86 C1 Drumsna
90 C3 Duagh
89 E3 Dublin
89 E4 Duleek
89 E3 Dunboyne
89 D1 Duncormick
87 E1 Dundalk
91 D1 Dunderrow
87 E2 Dundrum
86 C4 Dunfanaghy
87 D2 Dungannon
89 D2 Dungarvan
88 C1 Dungarvan
87 D3 Dungiven
86 B3 Dungloe
(An Clochan Liath)
91 D2 Dungourney
86 B3 Dunkineely
89 E3 Dun Laoghaire
89 D3 Dunlavin
87 E1 Dunleer
87 E3 Dunloy
90 C2 Dunmanway
89 E4 Dunmore
89 D1 Dunmore East
87 E2 Dunmurry
89 D4 Dunshauglin
88 C2 Durrow
90 B1 Durrus
88 B4 Dysart

E

86 A2 Easky
89 D3 Edenderry
88 C4 Edgeworthstown
87 D3 Eglinton
86 B1 Eiphin
87 D2 Emyvale
89 D3 Enfield
90 C4 Ennis
89 D2 Enniscorthy
85 F3 Enniscrone
90 C2 Enniskean
87 D2 Enniskillen
90 C4 Ennistymon
88 B3 Eyrecourt

F

86 C1 Farnaght
90 B2 Farranfore
91 D4 Feakle
86 C1 Fenagh
88 C3 Ferbane
91 D2 Fermoy
89 E2 Ferns
88 C2 Fethard
89 D1 Fethard
86 C1 Finnea
87 D2 Fintona
87 D2 Fivemiletown
89 D3 Fontstown
85 F3 Foxford
90 C3 Foynes
90 C3 Freemount
86 B1 Frenchpark
87 D3 Freshford
88 B4 Fuerty

G

91 D3 Galbally
85 F1 Galway
86 C2 Garrison
89 E4 Garristown
87 D3 Garvagh
88 C3 Geashill
87 E2 Gilford
90 C1 Glandore
91 D2 Glanworth
89 D2 Glaslough
88 C4 Glassan
88 B4 Glenamaddy

87 E3	Glenarm
87 E3	Glenavy
90 B2	Glenbeigh
86 B3	Glencolumbkille (Gleann Cholm Cille)
89 E3	Glendalough
89 E2	Glenealy
89 E2	Glengarriff
89 D1	Glenmore
86 B3	Glenties
90 C3	Glin
85 E2	Glinsk (Glinsce)
88 B2	Golden
90 B1	Goleen
89 D2	Goresbridge
89 E2	Gorey
88 A3	Gort
87 D3	Gortin
89 D2	Gowran
89 D2	Graiguenamanagh
86 C1	Granard
86 B2	Grange
87 F2	Greyabbey
89 E3	Greystones
87 E3	Gulladuff

H

89 D2	Hacketstown
85 E2	Headford
91 D3	Herbertstown
87 E2	Hillsborough
87 E2	Hilltown
91 D3	Hospital
88 C2	Holycross
87 F3	Holywood
89 E3	Howth

I

90 B2	Inch
90 C2	Inchigeelagh
91 D2	Inishannon
86 C2	Irvinestown

J

| 88 C2 | Johnstown |

K

90 C2	Kanturk
86 B2	Keadue
87 D2	Keady
85 D3	Keel
90 C2	Keenagh
87 E3	Kells
89 D4	Kells
90 B2	Kenmare
86 C2	Kesh
88 C3	Kilbeggan
89 D4	Kilberry
91 D1	Kilbrittain
86 B3	Kilcar (Cill Charthaigh)
89 D3	Kilcock
88 A3	Kilcolgan
88 B3	Kilconnell
89 E3	Kilcoole
88 C3	Kilcormac
89 D3	Kilcullen
87 E1	Kilcurry
89 D3	Kildare
89 D2	Kildavin
91 D3	Kildorrery
90 C4	Kilfenora
90 C2	Kilgarvan
90 B4	Kilkee
87 E1	Kilkeel
86 B1	Kilkelly
89 D2	Kilkenny
85 E1	Kilkieran
90 C3	Kilkinlea
88 C1	Kill
90 C3	Kiladysert
85 E3	Kilala
91 D4	Killaloe
90 C2	Killarney
88 C4	Killashee
88 C3	Killeigh
88 C2	Kilenaule
86 C1	Killashandra
90 C3	Killimer
88 B3	Killimor
89 E3	Killiney
89 E1	Killinick
90 B2	Killorglin
87 F2	Killough
89 D4	Killucan
86 B3	Killybegs
87 F2	Killyleagh
89 E3	Kilmacanoge
86 C4	Kilmacrenan
88 C1	Kilmacthomas
88 C1	Kilmaganny
85 E2	Kilmaine
91 D3	Kilmallock
88 C2	Kilmanagh

88 C1	Kilmeadan
89 D3	Kilmeage
89 E3	Kilmeedy
90 C2	Kilmichael
89 D1	Kilmore Quay
87 D1	Kilnaleck
87 E3	Kilrea
90 C3	Kilrush
88 C1	Kilsheelan
89 D2	Kiltealy
89 D2	Kiltegan
85 F2	Kiltimagh
88 C4	Kiltoom
89 D2	Kingscourt
86 B2	Kinlough
89 D4	Kinnegad
88 C3	Kinnitty
91 D1	Kinsale
85 F1	Kinvarra
87 F2	Kircubbin
86 A1	Knock
88 B4	Knockcroghery
88 C1	Knocklofty
89 D2	Knocktopher

L

90 C4	Lahinch
89 E3	Laragh
87 F3	Larne
90 B2	Lauragh
88 B3	Laurencetown
90 C1	Leap
85 E2	Leenane
89 D2	Leighlinbridge
86 C1	Leitrim
89 E3	Leixlip
88 C1	Lemybrien
85 D2	Letterfrack
86 C3	Letterkenny
86 C3	Lifford
87 D4	Limavady
91 D3	Limerick
86 C2	Lisbellaw
87 E2	Lisburn
90 C4	Liscanor
91 D3	Liscarroll
85 E1	Lisdoonvarna
88 C1	Lismore
86 C2	Lisnaskea
88 C4	Lisryan
90 C3	Listowel
90 C3	Loghill
87 D3	Londonderry
86 C1	Longford
87 E2	Loughbrickland
87 D2	Loughgall
86 B1	Loughglinn
88 B3	Loughrea
85 E2	Louisburgh
89 E3	Lucan
87 E2	Lurgan
89 E4	Lusk

M

90 C2	Macroom
87 D3	Maghera
87 E3	Maghera
87 D3	Magherafelt
86 C2	Maguiresbridge
89 E3	Malahide
87 D4	Malin
86 B3	Malin More
91 D2	Mallow
86 B2	Manorhamilton
87 E2	Markethill
89 D3	Maynooth
87 E2	Mazetown
87 D2	Middletown
91 D2	Midleton
86 C4	Milford
90 C2	Millstreet
90 B2	Milltown
90 C4	Milltown Malbay
88 C3	Mitchelstown
86 C1	Mohill
87 D2	Monaghan
89 D3	Monasterevin
88 C2	Moneygall
87 D3	Moneymore
88 B3	Monivea
88 C1	Mooncoin
87 E3	Moorfields
88 B4	Mount Bellew
86 B3	Mount Charles
88 C3	Mountmellick
88 C3	Mountrath
91 D4	Mountshannon
87 D4	Moville
87 D2	Moy
87 D1	Moynalty
88 C4	Moyvore
90 C2	Muckross
87 D4	Muff
89 D1	Mullinavat
88 C4	Mullingar
85 E3	Mulrany
89 D2	Myshall

N

89 D3	Naas
89 E4	Naul
85 D4	Navan
85 E2	Neale
91 D4	Nenagh
87 D2	Newbliss
89 D3	Newbridge (Droichead Nua)
87 E2	Newcastle
90 C3	Newcastle West
88 C1	Newinn
90 C3	Newmarket
90 C4	Newmarket-on-Fergus
85 E3	Newport
91 D3	Newport
89 D1	New Ross
87 E2	Newry
89 D2	Newtown
87 E3	Newtownabbey
87 F3	Newtownards
86 C2	Newtownbutler
87 D2	Newtownhamilton
89 E3	Newtownmount-kennedy
87 D3	Newtownstewart
86 C1	Newtown Forbes
87 D1	Nobber

O

89 D1	Oilgate
87 D1	Oldcastle
87 D3	Omagh
87 E2	Omeath
91 D3	Oola
88 A3	Oranmore
85 E2	Oughterard
91 D2	Ovens

P

91 D3	Pallas Green (New)
90 B2	Parknasilla
85 E2	Partry
89 D1	Passage East
91 D2	Passage West
91 D3	Patrickswell
89 D2	Paulstown
86 C3	Pettigo
87 D3	Plumbridge
87 D3	Pomeroy
87 F2	Portaferry
89 D3	Portarlington
87 F2	Portavogie
87 E3	Portglenone
88 C3	Portlaoise
89 E3	Portmarnock
89 E4	Portrane
91 D4	Portroe
87 D4	Portrush
87 E3	Portstewart
88 B3	Portumna
90 C2	Poulgorm Bridge
87 E2	Poyntzpass

R

89 D4	Raharney
87 E3	Randalstown
87 E3	Rasharkin
89 E3	Rathangan
91 D2	Rathcoole
91 D2	Rathcormack
88 C2	Rathdowney
89 E2	Rathdrum
87 E2	Rathfriland
90 C3	Rathkeale
86 C4	Rathmelton
89 D4	Rathmolyon
90 C2	Rathmore
86 C4	Rathmullan
89 E3	Rathnew
88 C4	Rathowen
89 D2	Rathvilly
89 E4	Ratoath
86 C4	Ray
91 E2	Ring (An Rinn)
91 D2	Ringaskiddy
87 D2	Rockcorry
86 C1	Roosky
86 C4	Rosapenna
91 D2	Rosbercon
88 B4	Roscommon
88 C3	Roscrea
90 C1	Ross Carbery
86 C2	Rosscor
89 E1	Rosslare
89 E1	Rosslare Habour
87 D2	Rosslea
87 E2	Rostrevor
89 D2	Roundstone
89 E3	Roundwood
89 E4	Rush

S

86 C3	St Johnstown
87 E2	Saintfield
89 D3	Sallins
91 D4	Scarriff
90 C2	Scartaglen
87 E2	Scarva
88 B1	Schull
86 C1	Scramoge
87 D2	Seskinore
91 E2	Shanagarry
91 D2	Shanagolden
88 C3	Shannonbridge
87 D1	Shercock
89 E2	Shillelagh
88 C3	Shinrone
85 F2	Shrule
91 D4	Silvermines
86 C3	Sion Mills
91 D4	Sixmilebridge
89 E4	Skerries
90 C1	Skibbereen
89 E4	Slane
86 B2	Sligo
87 D2	Smithborough
90 B2	Sneem
85 E1	Spiddal (An Spideal)
87 D3	Stewartstown
89 D2	Stonyford
86 C3	Strabane
89 D3	Stradbally
87 D3	Stradone
86 B2	Strandhill
87 F2	Strangford
86 C3	Stranorlar
89 E3	Strokestown
89 D4	Summerhill
86 C2	Swanlinbar
87 D3	Swatragh
86 A1	Swinford
89 E3	Swords

T

89 D1	Taghmon
89 E1	Tagoat
90 B2	Tahilla
89 E3	Tallaght
88 B1	Tallow
88 B1	Tallowbridge
87 E2	Tandragee
88 C4	Tang
90 C3	Tarbert
88 C2	Templemore
88 C2	Templetouhy
87 E1	Termonfeckin
89 D2	Thomastown
88 C2	Thurles
89 D3	Timahoe
91 D1	Timoleague
89 E2	Tinahely
91 D3	Tipperary
86 B2	Tobercurry
90 B1	Toormore
88 B2	Toomyvara
91 D4	Tralee
88 C1	Tramore
89 D4	Trim
88 A4	Tuam
91 D4	Tuamgraney
91 D4	Tulla
88 C3	Tullamore
89 D2	Tullow
85 E3	Turlough
88 C3	Tyrellspass

U

| 88 C2 | Urlingford |

V

| 87 D1 | Virginia |

W

87 E2	Warrenpoint
89 D1	Waterford
91 D2	Watergrasshill
90 B2	Waterville
85 E2	Westport
89 E1	Wexford
91 D2	Whitegate
87 F3	Whitehead
89 E3	Wicklow
89 E2	Woodenbridge
91 D4	Woodford

Y

| 91 E2 | Youghal |